LIVING AMONG THE SWISS

Michael Wells Glueck

Authors Choice Press

San Jose New York Lincoln Shanghai

Living Among the Swiss

Authors Choice Press
an imprint of iUniverse, Inc.

For information address:
iUniverse, Inc.
5220 S. 16th St., Suite 200
Lincoln, NE 68512
www.iuniverse.com

ISBN: 0-595-24171-9

Printed in the United States of America

LIVING AMONG THE SWISS

This book is written in the spirit of satire, a constitutionally protected form of speech. All references to actual persons living or departed are purely intentional. The author has made every effort to eschew political correctness while remaining loosely within the boundaries of good taste.

This edition of *Living Among The Swiss* is dedicated to my former students of Latin language and literature at City College of New York. Inevitably, those whom I remember best are mostly female:

Naomi Cyperstein
Anita Goldschmidt
Natalie Meltzer
Diana Négron
Ronald Penn
Susan Kusinitz Schmale
Esther Schreiber
Rona Schwab
Sharon Zane
and the incomparable Eddie Metzger.

Introduction

There are several subscribers listed in the Zürich telephone directory under the name Wichser. This would be unremarkable were it not for the fact that the word is familiar from the subtitles accompanying English-language movies shown in Switzerland. These subtitles are rich in vernacular expressions, and the word in question – which originally meant 'waxer' or 'polisher' – frequently appears in them as the modern German equivalent of an extreme *Fluch*, or 'profanity', consisting of ten letters and beginning with the letter 'c', which Lenny Bruce was regularly arrested for using in his nightclub act.

A milder *Schimpfwort*, or 'swear word', seven letters in length, beginning with 'a' and referring to a nether orifice, is invariably translated in the subtitles as Trottel. While there are no Trottels in the Zürich directory, there are a number of Trotts, Trotters and, especially, Trottmanns.

Other amusing Germanic names encountered here are Schmucki, or 'little jewel': e.g. Martin Schmucki owns a Mitsubishi dealership in Effretikon; Staub, which means 'dust', and which seems appropriate in a city that has an apparently Irish-owned employment agency named McDust; Fertig, or 'finished'; Frech, or 'bold'; Spiess, or 'skewer'; Schade, or 'shame'; Hinder, which means what it sounds like; and that of my Austrian barber, Stoss, which means 'shove'. T.S. Eliot's 'hollow men' are represented here by the surname Hohl. Siemens is a worldwide engineering firm, Wolfhard a male given name. I once went to an especially aggressive dentist named Jäger, which means 'hunter'. A macho Swiss named Köbi Boner owns an excellent ski shop in Klosters. He is ably assisted by his brother, Peter Boner. His countrymen include those named Fink, or 'Finch', and Finkbeiner, or 'Finchlegs', but not Dreckfink, which means 'guttersnipe'. Steiger, or 'climber', is a common name; Schwendler, or 'swindler', somewhat less so. My own name, which means 'good luck' or 'fortune', is hilarious to many Swiss, who invariably spell it by substituting an umlaut over the 'ü' in place of the following 'e'. The word for bad luck, *Pech*, does not appear as a surname in any Swiss telephone book.

There is also a surprising degree of correspondence between surnames and functions. Many smiths are named Schmid; a number of shoemakers, Schumacher or Schuhmacher. I purchased an automobile from a salesman named Händler, which means 'dealer'. My landlady is named Pfeiffer – no, not the actress – and every month I have to pay the piper. If I ever meet a Wichser I intend to run in the opposite direction.

To be sure, there are weird American names as well. Among those of Teutonic origin is that of a former network news anchorman, now retired, who is called by what appears to be a corrupted spelling of the German word *Krankheit*, 'illness'. A close friend of mine is misnamed Nancy Gross, and I once knew an investment analyst at Merrill Lynch named Fran Blech. Since her surname in German means 'pan' (or 'gutter', but never mind), I thought of her as 'Fran the Pan', or Frangipani. One of the U.S. television networks employs a financial commentator surnamed Insana. *Mens sana in corpore Insanae*. On the Anglo-Saxon side, we have our own Seamens as the name of a bank[1]. Then there was the shadowy figure from New Orleans named David Ferrie, who was cited in the conspiracy theory involving Lee Harvey Oswald. And lots of Irish-Americans are named Griffin, which the dictionary defines as a weird mythological monster, originally spelled gryphon.

Throughout Anglo-Saxon literature, of course, the use of 'charactonyms' is commonplace. Shakespeare created Shylock, Snub the Joiner, Bottom the Weaver, and Mistress Quickly. Fielding gave us the virtuous but misinformed Squire Allworthy, the villain Blifil and the ferule-wielding teacher Thwackum. Matthew Arnold bemoaned a newspaper headline describing a poor female miscreant only by her surname, Wragg. William Faulkner's Yoknapatawpha County was peopled with characters with such names as Workitt, which the author describes as a corruption of the English name Urquhart. Anyone who has read Fitzgerald's *The Great Gatsby* should remember the parade of appropriately named characters attending one of the hero's grand parties at 'West Egg', or Port Washington, Long Island. And Richard Russo recently created the memorable ne'er-do-well nicknamed Rub in his novel *Nobody's Fool*.

Ordinary names can also trigger exotic associations. In the early 1980s, I worked for a thrice-married Chaplinesque character named Midwood whom I thought of, according to my mood, as Dimwood, Wormwood, Peckerwood, or – even before he committed suicide – Deadwood. (The security analysts of San Francisco dedicated their subsequent annual report to his memory, doubtless out of guilt for having spurned him when he was available.) *De*

---

[1]In the 1950s, a venerable Cincinnati-based manufacturer of timepieces whose name was the German word for 'green' urged radio listeners: 'For Christmas and the whole New Year, give your spouse a marvelous Gruen!'

mortuis nil nisi bonum. Below our offices was a branch of Wells Fargo Bank where there worked an attractive customer representative named Curtice Poon, whom I always imagined marrying an accountant named Henry Tang. I once knew twin Japanese-American girls named Yoshi and Toshi. A prominent doctor in Nantucket is surnamed Lepore, which stems from the Latin word for hare, and on this island there is also a dentist whose surname appears to be a corrupted rendering of 'chien vert', or green dog. And in a previous life, when I was a university instructor of English and classical literature, my students included Peggy Willing and David Lovely.

German-Swiss place names can also be amusing to persons of different cultures. Examples: Horgen is a town on the lake of Zürich; Bitsch is a village in the Valais; and near Savognin on the Julierpass, there is a hamlet called Cunter.[2]

Ordinary German words can also titillate the uninitiated. Nobby Noblit, my genial innkeeper in Nantucket, likes to cite his favorite German word, *Mehrfahrtenkarten*, which refers to tickets valid for several trips on a train or bus. Similarly, a race car performing a qualifying lap around the track is making a *Wettfahrt*. My own favorites are mammary: a brassiere is a *Büstenhalter*, while pendulous breasts are called *Hängetitten*. *Pinkeln* does not refer to the color pink, for which the German word is *rosa*, but is an onomatopoetic verb meaning to urinate, tinkle, pinkle. The supermarket chain Migros used to sell a

---

[2]Note the comparative degree. By this logic, an American beauty pageant would be known, in the superlative, as a cuntest. The word *cunt* punned on by Hamlet when he teases Ophelia about 'country manners' stems from Latin *cunnus* through old French *queynte*, which appears in Chaucer's Canterbury Tales and from which the English word 'quaint' also derives. Thus, in an etymological sense, the phrase 'a quaint cunt' is redundant!

powdered detergent strengthener called *Wé-Wé*. *Schmuck* (which rhymes with 'brook') and *Putz* (same vowel sound) mean, respectively, jewel and treasure or finery; a jewelry box is a *Schmuckkästchen*, while a store specializing in antique jewelry will display a sign advertising *Antiker Schmuck*. Even some Swiss recognize the humor in this: a make-your-own jewelry shop in Zürich's old town is called *Schmuck It Yourself*. As a verb, *putzen* has another meaning, 'to clean', and a maid who dusts is called a *Putzmädchen*, which does not mean a handmaiden in any sense.

I am also bemused by the difference that the presence or absence of an umlaut can make. *Osterei* means Easter egg; *Österreich* is Austria. *Fordern* is a verb signifying to demand; *fördern*, however, means to further or advance a plan, assignment, or argument. *Schwül* refers to humid or sticky weather; *schwul* denotes homosexual. A *Vogel* is a bird; the plural is *Vögel*; one or more little birds are *Vögelein*; *Vögele* is the name of a low-priced chain of clothing stores; but *vögeln* – a staple component of the subtitles – means to fornicate.[3]

The names of Swiss businesses can prove rather tricky. Take, for example, the German name of the largest commercial bank in the country, and the last one to lose its triple-A rating: *Schweizerische Bankgesellschaft*. One remembers from high school or college German that *Gesellschaft* means company or society, so one concludes that this is the German name of the Swiss Bank Corporation.

Similarly, a visitor confronting a branch of *Schweizerischer Bankverein*, and recalling that the German name for the United States is *die Vereinigte Staaten*, readily translates this as Union Bank of Switzerland. After all, 'United' and 'Union' are similar, right?

---

[3] *Bumsen, ficken*, and *lecken* are synonyms of *vögeln*.

Well, no. Actually, the interpretations are incorrect in both instances. The German word for union is *Verband*, not *Verein*, which means association, although your dictionary may not make this distinction. *Bankgesellschaft* is Union Bank of Switzerland, whose officers' careers often parallel their promotions in the Swiss army. *Bankverein* is the Swiss Bank Corporation, the most liberal of the three *Grossbanken*; like the third member of this grouping, *Credit Suisse*, it lost its triple-A rating from both Moody's and, a few years later, Standard & Poors despite massive restructuring in the interim which maximized the benefits to profits of falling interest rates and produced annual earnings growth of at least forty percent before the second shoe fell.

This book describes the author's experiences during the past eight years of living and working among the Swiss. It examines several aspects of the Swiss banking system from the viewpoints of consumers, investors and employees. It depicts cultural differences as well as the practical difficulties confronting the new immigrant as he seeks to put down roots. It undertakes to edify the vicarious traveler as well as those seriously considering relocation here. Finally, it celebrates in some detail the beauty of this relatively simple and honest land, with especial emphasis on the cantons of Berner Oberland, Graubünden, and Wallis, as well as the environs of Zürich. While the observations focus on the German-Swiss, they are surprisingly applicable to the French- and Italian-speaking cantons as well.

Chapter I
Making the Initial Adjustment

If you have come to Switzerland to live, you are either related to a Swiss *Bürger;* or citizen; or you are independently wealthy, as evidenced by the ownership of property allotted to foreigners, such as an apartment acquired by subscription to the construction or renovation of a multi-family dwelling; or you have already secured a position in the workforce.

In the first two cases, the *Fremdenpolizei*, or foreigners' police, who are invariably women (the one who deals with my dossier is named Männle, or 'little man', i.e. 'virago') will issue you a Type 'C' residence permit, or *Niederlassungsbewilligung*, which is valid for ten years and indefinitely renewable, provided that you continue to demonstrate ample means – ample because it is quite expensive to live here. This type of permit, in contrast to the others, is issued not by a canton but by the federal government in Bern and thus entitles you to live and work anywhere in the country, to form your own company, to perform freelance work and even as noted, to own property – again, if you can afford it. Fully ninety percent of the inhabitants of this mountainous country rent their dwellings. Marrying a Swiss will not accelerate your eligibility for a 'C' permit – which for an American now takes five years, reduced from ten as of 1st January, 1996, thanks to President Clinton – but it will permit you to own property or a business in your spouse's name. (The president, however, is more likely to be remembered as the hands-on chief executive whose alleged extramarital activities, when discovered, have conferred a new significance upon the word 'scrutiny', and as an environmentalist who wastes a perfectly good cigar by depositing it in what comedian Jay Leno claims he refers to ironically and affectionately as 'my little humidor'.[1] Actor Billy Crystal was prevented by the organizers of the 1998 Academy Award ceremonies from jocularly disclosing that President Clinton's favorite movie is *The Nine Commandments*. That seems to be a generous estimate.)

In the third case, you will be granted a work permit, or *Aufenthaltsbewilligung*, of which there are two types: seasonal (or Type 'A'), which requires you to leave the country for three months each year unless you can show that it would be dangerous to go home (e.g. to Bosnia until recently) and that you have no other destination; or annual (Type 'B'), which can be renewed until you are eligible for a Type 'C' permit.

At the airport upon your arrival you will be given a chest x-ray and be asked to wait for the results. If you have an employer, he will already have commissioned a thorough physical examination before offering you a contract. Until you find permanent housing, you will stay in a hotel or, if working, in a simple apartment rented by your new firm. You will notice that I have omitted the category of staying with friends for the simple reason that such friends are harder to find in Switzerland than in any other European country. Even many Swiss characterize their countrymen as *ein verschlossenes Volk*, a closed society.

---

[1] A joke currently making the rounds has it that Gennifer Flowers, when asked whether her experiences were similar to those reported by Monica Lewinsky, replied, 'Close, but no cigar!'

Finding an apartment can be surprisingly difficult. The more reasonably priced ones are almost impossible for a foreigner to secure. Whereas in the U.S. the first financially qualified applicant must be granted a lease, in Switzerland the owner can indulge his preferences and prejudices as much as he likes. For example, I responded to one newspaper ad by telephone and heard a recording that ended, 'We don't want any Italians.' Other ads may ask you to write to a box number (answers are the exception) or to appear on, say, Thursday evening at seven. When you arrive you are likely to find thirty Swiss there ahead of you, and your chances of being chosen are virtually nil.

The most productive methods are to use your employer's House Commission, if he has one, which lists available rentals, or to go to an agency, often paid for by your employer. In Zürich, I recommend Büro Domino, up by the university. You will probably have to pay at least twice the price of the reasonable unit sought by the thirty Swiss, but it will have 'luxuries' which are standard in the U.S.: a deep freezer, a washing machine (and perhaps a dryer, here called a *Tumbler*) in the basement, and maybe even a dishwasher, known as a *Geschirrspüler*. No security deposit will be required once the owner has verified your employment and income. Your rent will fluctuate with the short-term interest rates upon which the owner's mortgage, if any, is probably based; there are no fixed mortgage rates longer than five years in Switzerland. In addition to rent, you will be required to pay a pro rata share (measured by cubic meters) of the cost of heating the building, as well as other expenses or *Nebenkosten* for providing hot water, cleaning the stairwell and basement, and general maintenance of the property. Gas and electric bills will arrive separately, and you will be issued an electronic key which routes to your electric meter the power used to run the shared washer (and dryer).

While, in contrast to the German custom, your new *pied-à-terre* will have a stove with oven, a refrigerator and, if a luxury unit, a deep freezer that looks like a food storage cabinet, do not expect it to have carpeting, window or door screens, air conditioning, lighting fixtures, (i.e. chandeliers) or closets. I have never seen screens in Switzerland, despite the presence in summer of a wide range of insects, and air conditioning is limited to a few offices, generally those of the higher-ups. A new unit will seldom have closets or lighting fixtures, and, in the case of an older unit, unless you are very lucky the previous tenant will have taken them along. For about one thousand Swiss francs you can buy attractive and reasonably priced woolen rugs at Huser on Agnesstrasse. Four of the least expensive armoire kits at Ikea in Spreitenbach or Dietikon outside of Zürich will cost eight hundred Swiss francs, and you can figure on spending another one thousand, two hundred Swiss francs or so on simple lighting fixtures with installation. Do not attempt to connect fixtures to the wires you see hanging from the ceiling unless you are sure you know how to turn off the voltage, as a shock of two hundred and twenty volts can ruin your day.

Except in Zermatt, I have never encountered do-it-yourself launderettes in Switzerland. Your basement machine will run off a dial or metal punch card, with various programs to select from. As with a dishwasher, the longest of these takes seventy-five minutes, and maximum cycle time on a dryer is ninety minutes. Most Swiss, being thrifty, shun dryers, preferring to hang their clothes in the basement and thus avoid linting. Because of the relatively long cycle times and the paucity of machines – usually one per house – your *Hauswart* or superintendent may assign you one evening per week to do your laundry, or he may post a sign-up calendar. When you are finished using the washing machine, you are expected to clean and dry both the soap container and the drain plug, and to leave them conspicuously shiny on top of the machine.

You can avoid this regimentation by purchasing a combination washer or dryer. These run from one thousand to three thousand Swiss francs new, and are also available (often at the same store, e.g. Fust on Hottingerplatz) used, with a guarantee. The disadvantage of this, of course, is the bathroom crowding that will result from the machine and its various hoses and connections.

Whichever machine you use, it is imperative to set the temperature far below the maximum of ninety degrees Celsius, which is near the boiling point. Most clothes purchased here have labels that indicate maximum temperatures, which can be as low as thirty degrees Celsius for ski jackets. Above this level colors fade and fabrics shrink, especially those purchased over here, where mercerizing is known but Sanforizing simply does not exist!

Except in such places as Zermatt, when you are away from home you will have to pay by the piece for laundry and dry cleaning, and items you expect to be washed (such as a down ski parka) may wind up being dry-cleaned, which costs more – about forty Swiss francs. In major cities there are discount dry cleaners that charge six or seven francs per item, but I have never ventured to try one of these. 'Shirt service' currently costs about six francs per dress shirt almost anywhere. When you bring your shirts, you will not be given a receipt, nor will your item count be confirmed: trust is the basis of this commercial relationship, as of so many others in Switzerland.

Do not worry about theft from the basement clothes lines; it doesn't happen here. Especially in smaller apartment buildings, with one dwelling per floor, many Swiss hang their coats and store their shoes and boots on the landing outside their front door. Baby carriages can often be found just inside the main entrance to the building; laundry products and bicycles are stored in open basements.

Honesty is simply presumed here, and it has been elevated into a basic legal principle, known as *treu und glauben*, full faith and credit, which applies to acts of commission and omission. Business letters almost invariably begin with *Sehr geehrte/r Frau/Herr*, 'Most Honorable Madam/Sir', subtly reminding the recipient of the accepted standard of behavior. As in English, the words for 'honor' and 'honest' are etymologically related. Never show a Swiss that you distrust or disbelieve him, as he or she will immediately conclude that you are projecting your own flawed character (here thought of as 'tricky', in the English word adopted for this purpose). If, for example, you wish to peruse a contract written in German legalese before signing it, proceed very carefully: even if your suspicions prove to be justified, you are traversing a minefield.

If you wish to use U.S. appliances which run only on one hundred and ten volts of alternating current, you will need about one thousand Swiss francs worth of step-down transformers. Now that a Zürich landmark, the Mattern electronics store near Central, has passed into history, these are available at Mattern's successor, Pustella Elektronik on Holstrasse 58 near the Langstrasse. There can also purchase a couple of dozen converter plugs, and one four-pronged telephone plug for each American telephone. (These are also available at Electro Bietenholz on Hottingerplatz, and you can connect these yourself: cut off the alligator clips, strip an inch of outer insulation, and connect the inner wires by color code to the side screws of the four-prong.) It is advantageous to bring a U.S. phone because most Swiss varieties lack a switch to turn off the bell, this being a service provided by the telephone company at a charge, as is an itemized bill.

Some recent models do enable you to block the line or silence the bell by pressing a combination of buttons, but it is then impossible to tell at a glance whether the unit is on or off. All enable you to choose between pulse and tone, and some have one-way speakers through which you can hear but not speak – a take-off of the old French phones with two receivers. Some models also feature counters which keep track of how much you are spending as you talk. At the official post office store, the colors are limited: black, white, dark green or black with a royal blue receiver. Additional choices are available at private stores. In general, prices are coming down toward U.S. levels. At Classic Telephone on Mühlebachstrasse, the proprietor, Herr Engler, will sell you an analog Brazilian model with an on-off switch.

You should also bring an answering machine, as the U.S. prices are far below the Swiss ones. Be sure to choose a model which allows you to retrieve your calls from remote locations with a beeper. If the machine has this capacity but doesn't come with a beeper, Radio Shack or competing electronic outlets will sell you one for around five dollars. You will need a beeper in Switzerland because the push-button telephones which finally appeared here at the end of the 1980s do not all emit standard touch tones. Some are analog, including many coin telephones; others emit a peep of identical pitch for every digit dialed. The truly digital, touch-tone pay phones generally have one slot for all coins above five centimes, instead of four slots for either ten, twenty, fifty centimes and a franc, or for ten, twenty centimes, one franc, and five francs. Most post offices have these, but the ones *inside* often stop emitting tones after the dialed number is answered, while the coin phones outside, if touch-tone, do not have this limitation.

More and more pay phones now accept a plastic 'Taxcard' loaded with five, ten, or twenty francs, and available (naturally) at post offices and train stations. In 1998 the directories inside the booths began to be replaced by electronic 'telephone books' which offer a choice of four languages and which can dial the located number automatically.

You should bring your furniture, including the TV and VCR. Although the former will not work here on a stand-alone basis, by introducing a transformer you can use the combination to play American-format (NTSC) movies, available in video rental stores (sometimes before the film arrives at the local theaters, which can take up to six months after release in the U.S.). At Seeholzer in Zürich or Media Markt in nearby Dietikon you can purchase a JVC or Panasonic VCR which converts NTSC-formatted VHS movies into the PAL format used in Europe, and which also plays PAL tapes, for anywhere from six hundred and ninety Swiss francs to one thousand, five hundred Swiss francs. (For twice the higher amount you can buy a true multi-format VCR which also includes the Japanese standard.)

Eventually, you will need to buy a TV here. Smaller Sony models are available for under nine hundred Swiss francs (stereo – the mono version is two hundred Swiss francs less) which accept NTSC video input. For a full-sized, top-of-the-line Sony, with Panasonic VCR and a glass and wrought iron table, you will have to lay out about three thousand Swiss francs, but it will be worth it, as the definition and illusion of depth are superior. The remote control unit also functions as an optical scanner which reads bar codes on a card provided by the cable company or installer for the purposes of programming channels on the TV. Such bar codes also appear in the local equivalents of *TV Guide*, thus enabling you to use the scanner to set recording times on the VCR.

One of the rare bargains in Switzerland is a satellite dish, available at Fust for three hundred Swiss francs and tuned to the Eutel or Astra (not RCA) satellites. The former will enable you to receive NBC and CBS broadcasts from the U.S. while the latter will add NBC's cable channel, CNBC, and Rupert Murdoch's unencrypted Sky News to the CNN and BBC channels available on the *Rediffusion* cable system, which monopolizes Zürich. (Some private cable systems, as in Zermatt, include Sky News.) Sky News carried the O.J. Simpson criminal trial live and sporadically shows *60 Minutes, A Current Affair*, and *Court TV* highlights, as well as the CBS and ABC network news shows. (You can tape them, of course, for more convenient viewing.) Via Astra you can also access Eurosports as well as local stations, although – apart from Saturday night specials – their fare, even including nudity, may not often suit your taste.

Unfortunately, Sky One (which features daily *Court TV* highlights and also broadcasts such U.S. soap operas as *Murder One*), Sky Sports, and Sky Movies, though audible via satellite, are not visible thanks to encryption, and you cannot subscribe from a Swiss address because the copyrights are not valid outside the United Kingdom and the Republic of Ireland. Eat your heart out. You can catch major boxing and other events broadcast via closed circuit by Sky Sports at the Oliver Twist pub, also known as Mr. Pickwick's, on Rindermarkt in the old town; reservations are highly advisable.

Your stereo will receive cable radio stations, including (in Zürich) the BBC World Service and the Voice of America, as well as those dedicated to classical music, of which Zürich has access to no fewer than eight, emanating from Austria, Germany and France as well as German Switzerland and the *Suisse Romande*, the French part of Switzerland. Do not subscribe to the post office's radio stations, which are received by many hotels, as the fidelity is poor, and the 'free' stations offer ample variety.

When you order a telephone line, with installation to be done by a private installer such as *Rediffusion*, the post office will ask you whether you have a TV or radio, and you must answer honestly and pay a monthly commission (about twelve Swiss francs for any and all radio reception, including a car or portable unit, and forty Swiss francs for TV and radio). You will also have to deposit up to one thousand Swiss francs for the telephone and not expect to recover it (with interest) for several years, until you have established a satisfactory record of payment.

When you apply for the telephone, you will have to supply your occupation or profession, which at your option can be listed alongside your name in the telephone book and information service. This feature helps you distinguish, for example, Esther Koch, the doctor's assistant, from a like-named person who is a musician or salesperson. When I applied for a telephone, I gave my profession as *Finanz Analytiker*, financial analyst, but checked the 'no' box for the option of including this information in the public record. The clerk who processed my application misread *Finanz* as *Franz.*, the abbreviation for *Französisch*, French. Ever thereafter, despite my written corrections, bills and other correspondence to me from the PTT (postal, telephone and telegraph service) have been addressed to Michael Glueck, French analyst. I'm not quite sure what such a profession entails, but if you should ever need one of its practitioners I suggest that you look elsewhere.

You should take advantage of the opportunity to purchase an Electrolux or Miele vacuum cleaner with an eleven hundred or twelve hundred volt motor for two hundred Swiss francs or so, although the upscale models can cost four times as much. The German word for this appliance – which you are unlikely to have learned at university – is *Staubsauger*, literally, 'dust sucker'.

If you live in Zürich, you must deposit your garbage, whether in dumpsters or in designated locations at the curb, in specially purchased 'Züri' sacks, which cost upwards of two Swiss francs apiece, depending on size. Use of any other container will result in a fine of one hundred Swiss francs for the first offense and escalating amounts thereafter. Because neighborhood cats and large hamster-like creatures called *Marder* like to tear open garbage bags left by the curb and strew their contents along the sidewalk, you should try to locate a nearby dumpster. I used one around the corner from my building for five years, until its owners finally installed a lock to discourage me from doing so.

At central locations there are large containers for aluminum cans, clear bottles, brown bottles and polyethylene terephthalate (PET) bottles. The Swiss practicing such recycling may well be wearing fur coats and alligator accessories.

A word about Swiss bathrooms. These are generally separate from WCs, although the latter contain small washbasins. Luxury bathrooms often have two contiguous washbasins, so that a couple can brush their teeth side by side. (My landlady was horrified when I suggested replacing one of the sinks with another toilet.) Your bathtub is unlikely to have a shower curtain or rod, which you must purchase. Shower doors must be ordered, will take about six weeks to arrive, and will cost approximately one thousand Swiss francs. Spirella is the best brand and comes in both sliding and folding varieties. A fixed shower head in the wall is far less common than a flexible hose and head, often with a wall bracket, and in any case the threads will not accommodate your Speakman or Water Pik head without an adapter, and even then the wall bracket may not be strong enough to hold a heavy version.

As for toilets, for a country that boasts a high standard of living, these can be surprisingly primitive, as is the toilet paper. (Fortunately, Kleenex and other comparable brands of facial tissue are readily available, and they all come in the familiar U.S. rectangular size that will fit your dispenser; do not, however, expect to find extra-large tissues here.) You will probably wish to replace the toilet seat locally, as even the luxury sizes may not be American Standard, and the thin plastic of standard issue can prove uncomfortable.

If you bring your car, as I did, do not drive it before an insurance agency here (I recommend *Berner Versicherung*) has had it registered and licensed (about six hundred Swiss francs per year). Expect to pay at least two thousand, four hundred Swiss francs for annual auto insurance including collision and after maximum discounts for a safe driving record, as documented by your previous U.S. insurance company which will supply such certification upon request. In addition to auto insurance, you will need to purchase a homeowner's policy (perhaps five hundred and fifty Swiss francs per year), and private liability (*Haftpflicht*) and lawyer's (*Rechtsschutz*) coverage for residence and auto (together, about two hundred and forty Swiss francs per year for substantial protection). When you leave Switzerland, the homeowner's policy will cover the cost of such repairs as filling in the holes in the walls where you hung pictures, as well as the unamortized portion of the assumed ten-year life of the interior paint.

You should also obtain through your insurance agent a booklet describing traffic signs and regulations; the former can be misleading. For example, a sign depicting two cars separated by a solid line and traveling in opposite directions means 'no passing', while a similar picture containing a diagonal line through these images means that the no passing zone is ending. Without a booklet, one is likely to attribute the reverse meanings to these signs.

Be warned that violations other than minor speeding can result in large fines and suspension of your license. There are automatic cameras at strategic intersections or stretches of highway that measure your speed or capture you going through a red light and, amazingly, no one ever shoots them out. The Swiss stopped mailing such pictures when spouses began inquiring about the identity of the driver's companion. (In the U.S. I have seen only one automated speed monitor, along the Maine Turnpike, and it only flashes a warning.)

Like other Europeans, the Swiss do not condone even minor contact between automobiles. You will have to learn to park and pull up to gasoline pumps without touching bumpers. If you slip in this regard, most Swiss will grimace and bear it, but a few will see an opportunity for venality and insist on calling a policeman to examine a non-existent scratch. This can take an hour, and may result in a reduction of your insurance discount for safe driving.

Within thirty days of the arrival of your car, you should visit the Motor Vehicle Department, or *Strassenverkehrsamt*, to exchange your driver's license for a Swiss one, valid until the age of seventy, with no periodic tests for vision or anything else if you are careful and lucky. Thereafter you must be certified by a physician every two years as having sufficiently quick reflexes and general good health to be permitted to continue driving. You will also need to make an appointment to have your car inspected for safety and required modifications. For example, the speedometer (but not necessarily the odometer) must read in kilometers, and the lights must conform to Swiss standards: parking lights must be inside the headlamp shields and all other front and side lamps can only be white (not yellow, as in France) flashing turn signal indicators. Do not be surprised if the third brake light in the rear window and any alarm system have to be removed.

You should not go to the inspection site yourself, as the officials are especially capricious toward foreigners. Instead, find a garage that services your make of car and let it prepare your car for the inspection (a process that includes washing the motor) and take it there. And do not be shocked at the prices: perhaps five hundred Swiss francs for preparation, another two hundred Swiss francs for the chauffeur service, and forty-eight Swiss francs for the inspection itself. Subsequent inspections are required every two years, as is an emissions test performed by your garage.

Although it can cost two thousand Swiss francs to make these changes, it is nonetheless worth it. All but the most basic new cars are prohibitively expensive here, and while the train service is legendary, you will need a car for convenience and, on longer trips, for efficiency: to drive from Zürich to Zermatt through the Lötschberg tunnel can take as little as three and a half hours, as opposed to five by train. Moreover, if you are not traveling alone, it is always less expensive to drive and pay parking fees than to purchase two train fares. One caveat: you must buy a windshield sticker in order to use any autobahn, at an annual cost of forty Swiss francs.

Most Swiss change their motor oil only once per year, since the country is small and the costs are high: one hundred Swiss francs for labor, plus the cost of the oil and filter. I recently took the car in for a change of motor oil, transmission fluid and respective filters, and the bill exceeded three hundred Swiss francs. Gasoline, here called *Benzin*, costs about SwFr 1.20 per liter – among the cheapest prices in Europe.

As you will have gathered by now, you should bring several thousand dollars when you arrive to defray the costs of settling in. If you do buy a car here, look for a used luxury model. The Swiss are reluctant to spend serious money on anything but a Mercedes or Beemer, and you can find used Honda Legends (the trademark *Acura* is not registered here) in mint condition with full service records for more reasonable prices, especially if you deal with an individual. Amusingly, most Swiss still prefer a 'classic' American car such as a Firebird to a Japanese luxury model; most of the Japanese cars you see here are smaller, less expensive varieties.

If your new dwelling doesn't have a garage, you can either rent one at two hundred Swiss francs per month or buy a neighborhood parking authorization from your local police station for two hundred and forty Swiss francs per year. It will be mailed to you in about a week and in the meantime you will have to keep your car parked off the streets, even if you have already had it licensed and insured. Your insurance agent or local police station will give you a parking 'wheel' or top-of-dashboard indicator for use when you are parking for a short time in other areas.

Let me return briefly to the alternative of traveling by train. While on winter weekends it can be safer than venturing out on roads full of German tourists driving aggressively on summer tires, and notwithstanding the spectacular views, it isn't as great as its reputation. In winter, the cars are often overheated and you may encounter opposition if you try to lower the thermostat in the coach you have chosen. The custom is that windows can be opened only when a train is standing in a station and, either as soon as you open one or the instant the train begins to move, another passenger (usually a little old lady) will ask you to close it. Even in first class, the odors of the tunnels will permeate your clothing. And in second class you will frequently encounter not only the harrowingly unpleasant odors of the great unwashed and undeodorized, but also the harsh and loud voices of children and adults afflicted with Down's syndrome, who are seldom institutionalized here.

A word about Swiss food. It is rich in carbohydrates and laden with high-calorie sauces. The Swiss hate baked potatoes but love *Rösti*, a version of cottage fries soaked in butter. The German-Swiss love fried foods, which are hard to digest and engender lots of gas (which all too often can simply not be suppressed: my own nether eructations usually become most urgent when I am riding on a crowded cable car or hiking past large families). Veal is far more popular than beef, and the favorite form is not *Wiener Schnitzel* (which can sometimes be made of pork) but the minced variety known as *Geschnetzeltes Kalbsfleisch*, often prefixed by *Züri* (for Zürich). A veal cutlet is known as a *Schnitzel*; *Kotelette* means chop. And *Lammnüsschen* are nuggets, not 'little lamb nuts' or testicles. When you are served a steak, it invariably comes with a large lump of seasoned butter on top, known as the *Café de Paris*. The larding on of saturated fats has resulted in, among other things, the highest rate of prostate cancer in Europe.

Amusingly, some of the resort hotels which serve this fare think that their kitchens are French, and print their menus accordingly. If calling *Wiener Schnitzel* '*Escalope de veau Viennoise*' converts it into French cuisine, then so be it. As the Jewish mother said when her son was baptized at the age of twenty-nine, 'Apple, apple, you're an orange.' Patrick Duffy, you're a Buddhist?[2]

A note about fruits and vegetables. The local markets offer many varieties of oranges – which, by the way, are called by that name, never by the High German word

---

[2]When he turned 21, a school acquaintance of mine, Yigael Goldfarb, successively and legally changed his name to Leon Goldfarb, then to Leon Kenman, and finally to Winston Carruthers. I telephoned one day, and his mother answered. 'May I speak with Winston Carruthers, please?' 'Just a minute. YIGAEL!'

Apfelsine – including Spanish and Moroccan (or Moro) blood oranges, which are wonderful, as well as Jaffa and blond oranges. The Moro and blond varieties are navel oranges, and therefore seedless. Never available are Californian navels; the Florida version sometimes appears. Mangoes and delicious Japanese persimmons, or *kakis*, abound everywhere. The finer markets offer Californian seedless grapes in late autumn; otherwise, all European grapes sold here seem to have seeds. *Maiskolben*, or corn on the cob, is almost always yellow (and usually quite tough), as the Swiss are suspicious of white corn.

An afterword about Swiss desserts. You probably are familiar with most of them, which derive from central European cuisines: *Schwarzwaldertorte*, or Black Forest pie; *Dobischtorte*; *Charlotte russe*; *Sabayon*, or custard laced with Madeira wine. But you may not have heard of *Tiramisu*, a spun-cheese delicacy made of Ricotta and Mascarpone; and your idea of a *Nesselrode Coupe* may not correspond to the Swiss reality. When I was a child in the Midwest, *Nesselrode* was a kind of fruited spumoni ice cream. But here it is a cloyingly sweet, spun chestnut confection, for which the German name is *Vermicel*, alluding to its resemblance to the thin pasta known as vermicelli. Spumoni, by the way, is known as *Stracciatella*. Biscuit tortoni does not exist. And a tartufo looks and tastes the same as in America.

In order to emulate the leanness of most Swiss, you will need to exercise restraint as well as your body.

A word about the additional adjustments that will have to be made by your dependents, if any. Apart from the strange customs and difficult dialects, and aside from readjusting to home and school, they – and especially a non-professional or non-working spouse – will face the problem of how to pass the time while you are working. Loneliness and depression are common in any foreign milieu, but especially in Switzerland where few burghers are *ausländerfreundlich*, friendly toward foreigners, and where invitations to dinner are extremely rare. I have frequently been an overnight or dinner guest in England, France, Holland, and Germany, but almost never in Switzerland. In order not to find your marriage severely tested you will need a spouse with the devotion of a Biblical Ruth. I myself have never found such a wife; and to judge from the relatively brief stay of most wholly American couples who venture to come here to live, my experience is far from atypical.

Chapter II
At Work Among the Swiss

Let us assume that your first job in Switzerland, as mine was, is with one of the three large, publicly owned Swiss banks. By custom, you will have signed an employment contract which specifies your initial salary, any bonus, mutual constraints on termination and general conditions of employment. You will be expected to work a minimum of forty-two hours per week, and below the level of assistant vice-president you will probably have to punch a time clock. The clock runs from eight in the morning until seven in the evening; if you arrive earlier or stay later you note these adjustments on a monthly time card, which is the vehicle for getting paid. Extra hours, even if not required, may be compensated in time, though not in money, at the end of each year, if your supervisor permits. I used to take off the week between Christmas and New Year's on this basis. You can also run as much as fifteen hours behind your monthly obligation and still be paid in full, but this feature should be used quite sparingly, if at all.

At the large banks the office is open on Saturdays, but not on Sundays. Then, as on weeknights, you must be prepared to show your identification card to a guard or risk serious embarrassment. At the private bank I subsequently worked for, only top officers entrusted with special keys could come in on Saturdays. My own key to the building, like most others, had a chip which limited the hours when it functioned. In any case, the host computer was turned off in the absence of EDP employees, so that no uploading of reports or estimates could be made. As you have probably gathered by now, the vaunted Swiss work ethic is not so formidable.

By law, every full-time employee in the country must receive a paid annual vacation of at least four weeks. If you are over fifty, or are a vice-president, you may be granted five weeks; if both, as many as six. Notice the use of the word 'granted' in the above sentence. In Switzerland, the gap between workers and bosses is quite large, and there is very little social mobility or room for entrepreneurship. Even during initial salary discussions, one does not attempt to negotiate anything, or to ask for anything extra, without serious risk of offending either a personnel official, to whom enormous power is delegated, or one's *Vorgesetzener* (immediate superior), or both. (I once asked for permission to take part of my compensatory free time during the first week in January instead of the last week in December, when it snowed in southern Florida, my destination, and this proved to be a surprisingly big deal, with permission reluctantly granted at the cost of considerable accumulated goodwill.) As in the U.S., vacation scheduling may have to be approved in advance to assure functional continuity.

In addition to vacations, there are paid holidays, which include: 26th December and 2nd January; Friday through Monday of Easter week; in Zürich, *Sechseläuten* in mid-April, when a straw 'snowman' is burned to celebrate the arrival of spring; *Auffahrt*, or Ascension; *Pfingsten*, or Whitsuntide; Swiss National Day on 1st August; and, again in Zürich, *Knabenschiessen* in mid-September, when little boys take target practice. If 1st August or another holiday (other than Christmas, New Year's, or Easter) falls on a Thursday, the next day is not a holiday and one must take a vacation day to make the 'bridge' to the weekend.

Businesses close early on the workday preceding most holidays, usually around four o'clock.

There is also an unofficial holiday in the early morning following the last day of school before Christmas when costumed children march through their neighborhoods banging drums, shooting off firecrackers, and spraying cars with shaving cream. This was called off in 1995, after previous demonstrations produced such vandalism as upended automobiles, but resumed without untoward incident in 1996. If your vehicle is parked on a Zürich street during this 'holiday', you would do well to remember the importance of washing off the shaving cream before it erodes the car's finish.

A note about terminology. Christmas is called *Weihnacht* or *Weihnachten*; New Year's Eve, *Silvester* or, equally acceptably, *Sylvester*. As in England, 26th December is known as *St. Stephenstag*, St. Stephen's Day, while 2nd January (also a holiday) is called *St. Berchtoldstag*, St. Berchtold's Day. The Thursday before Good Friday (itself called *Karfreitag*) is known as *Grüner Donnerstag*, Green Thursday, while Easter is *Ostern*. A special autumn Sunday Prayer Day is known as *Bettag*, which comes from *beten*, to pray, and *Tag*, day, not from *Bett* and *Tag*, 'Bed Day'.

Having discussed days off, let us turn to compensation. Although the German words *Gehalt* and *Salär*, salary, exist the Swiss invariably use the word *Lohn*, reward. If your contractual compensation includes a bonus it will be called, in bad etymology, a *Gratifikation*, or gratuity. Get the idea? You are essentially a servant. But you will have some protection against sudden job loss. Unless you have flagrantly violated your contract, at the AVP level two months' notification of termination by either side is required. At the VP level, which includes an expense allowance, three months' notice is typical at a large bank. (At most private banks, the requirements at these levels are, respectively, six months' and twelve months' notice.) Should you leave abruptly, you may have to pay the *employer* your regular salary for the dishonored term!

Annual salaries are typically divided into thirteen monthly installments, with half the pay for the extra month paid toward the end of June and the other half in either November or December. Thus, when interviewing it is a good idea to ascertain your *annual* salary, as your employer's personnel officer may not be above quoting a monthly salary with twelve installments rather than thirteen in mind.

If you are lucky, or a vice-president, you will have a private office. Once again, this must be voluntarily granted; it cannot be negotiated. If you are unlucky, you will have to endure the odors of cigarette or cigar tobacco, perspiration and stale clothing worn by your Swiss colleagues. You will also be exposed to the colds and influenza that they invariably bring back (along with malnutrition) from their mandatory three weeks of annual military service.

A typical Swiss youth starting out at a bank owns no suits and one or, at most, two sport jackets and has never in his lifetime frequented a dry cleaner. His mother, wife or girlfriend washes and irons his shirts, which may be homespun (like Ghandi's diaper in the movie of that name) and patched. He will don a tie, if he remembers, only when about to attend a presentation and if the shirt he happened to wear that day is a dress shirt. His socks, worn with such business attire as he possesses, are likely to be white. He is unlikely to be in the habit of daily showers and changes of underwear and socks, and he probably does not use deodorant. (Twice in my three years at Credit Suisse I sent flagrant stinkers a bar of deodorant soap and a stick of deodorant through the interoffice mail; in more than twenty years of working in the U.S. I had to do this only once.) Only the head of the research department changed his shirt every day.

Despite these odors, which are often exacerbated by heavy intakes of garlic, it is a good idea to bring a hook to the office and fasten it to the back of the door so that you do not have to hang your jacket and outer coat in the same closet as the musty, vintage garments of your colleagues.

Except for the head of your department, who will probably have a doctorate, and other officers who may have a baccalaureate but not a master's degree, none of your colleagues is likely to have had a university education. The typical Swiss banking employee has had either a six-month *Lehre* or *Praktikum* (apprenticeship) or even a couple of years of business school, and he probably has rudimentary computer skills, but he is unlikely to be able to construct a spreadsheet macro or to screen a database.

In the large banks, there are subsidized employee cafeterias, and your coworkers will both welcome and expect your company at lunch. For six to eight francs you will be nourished, but not luxuriously. A frequent menu item is *Kaninchen*, which brings dog meat to mind but actually means 'rabbit'. Roast saddle of rabbit is rendered as *Gebratenes Kaninchenkeule*, literally roast anus of rabbit: *keule* is etymologically equivalent to the Spanish word *culo*, which means hole, anus, or, by synecdoche, buttocks. A kind of hominy, or a version of chick peas, called 'polenta', which I usually confuse with 'placenta', is often served. At Christmas, there will be a decent meal and every two years there will be a departmental outing to a lake or mountain, with good drinking but only cold cuts or snacks to eat.

A weak union represents all Swiss banking employees. Even though you have not joined it – nor will you be asked to – your annual salary increases will be the standard three or four percent regardless of your performance, or the bank's. There are no real incentives at the large banks. After two or three years, you may receive a small premium or bonus of two to three thousand francs. And once you attain a certain level, the union agreement may exclude you from participating in the annual salary increase.

Nonetheless, you will be paid well by U.S. standards, and as long as you show up for work on time and put in the required hours, you are unlikely to be fired, at least in the initial years. You need your employer's permission to change jobs, or your department head's permission to change departments. These will almost certainly not be granted during the first year, and you will be expected to remain at least three years before requesting such permission. Correspondingly, no final judgment on your performance will be made for at least three years.

The large banks, though they lack significant performance incentives, tend to attract relatively unambitious employees who value the comparative job security. Such coworkers do not make bad colleagues: they don't pose formidable competition or lust after your job, they are far less political than private bankers and, on the whole, they are happier and more contented. Most of them marry and have two children, and they take advantage of the subsidized offerings such as inexpensive wristwatches, one or two weekend ski trips and a couple of classical concerts per year. Yet they still manage to save a proportion of their income that would astound the typical U.S. white-collar worker. Partly this is because the banks do pay quite generously compared with other institutions in Switzerland as well as with their counterparts in the U.S.

How well can you expect to be paid? Well, in 1989 my twenty-six year old assistant, with two years' of computer school, was hired for sixty-six thousand Swiss francs per year, and one month later a major private bank offered him ninety-seven thousand Swiss francs! Today, he is a highly prized analyst at this bank, and at the age of thirty-three he earns as much as I did after three years in Switzerland. How much was that? Well, I began over the six-figure threshold, which I had never achieved in the U.S., and within three years, thanks to salary increases geared to inflation and the depreciation of the U.S. dollar against the Swiss franc, I had nearly doubled my last U.S. salary.

(Lest you lick your lips in envy, consider how little one hundred Swiss francs, currently about sixty-five dollars, will buy at my local Coop supermarket: eight chicken legs and thighs, two four-bone racks of lamb, one small lamb filet, two liters of milk, eight tomatoes, eight carrots, four red peppers, eight navel blood oranges, and four pears. U.S. tenderloin, which to my taste is far superior to the Swiss and French *Charolais* varieties that are also available here, costs nine francs per hundred grams [about 0.22 pounds]. So nine tenths of a pound of filet mignon, or just over four hundred grams, would cost about thirty-six Swiss francs, or twenty-four dollars!)

You will notice that most of your coworkers are quite young – as, most probably, are you. After the age of forty, poor performance is regarded more seriously, and after fifty you become expendable. As a newspaper headline recently reminded readers, lifetime employment is history. Almost no one is permitted to work beyond normal retirement age, which (except for such pension providers as Zürich Insurance Company) is steadily being reduced toward sixty, or even fifty-five. Credit Suisse permits retirement with full pension at the age of sixty-four; Swiss Reinsurance, at the age of sixty.

By implication, your mobility as you age becomes increasingly limited, even though pension accounts became portable at the beginning of 1995. Newspaper advertisements for employees usually specify an 'ideal' age, generally twenty-five to thirty-five, with an upper limit of forty or forty-five for positions requiring experience. (A familiar Swiss joke is that the ideal employee is twenty years old with thirty years' experience.) For example, a headhunter recently ran an ad seeking both a private banker and a portfolio manager. The former, who will handle client relations, should be thirty-five to forty-five; the latter, who will actually manage the funds, should be thirty to forty! Some ads specify sex by adding the suffix -*in* to the description of the person sought, as in *Sachbearbeiterin*, mid-level female employee; others may actually request a photograph! U.S. lawyers would have a field day here if Title VII laws were universally in force.

Partially because of this bias toward youth, the social safety net is generous. Unemployment compensation in its various forms lasts just over two years, and you are eligible for it after having worked an equal length of time here – even if you left your job voluntarily. Maximum compensation for a single person amounts to fifty-two thousand dollars per year; for a head of household, about ten percent more. In the last six months, the monthly compensation decreases by one thousand Swiss francs, ceases to be taxable and involves a bit more red tape to receive. At that point, moreover, six-month work programs and assistance in finding a new position are offered, but these are generally at the bottom rung of the employment ladder and they pay no more than four thousand Swiss francs per month, fully taxable, which is not enough to live independently in Switzerland, or at least in Zürich.

Throughout the 1980s, the Swiss job market was booming, and qualified foreigners of mature age and experience were welcome, often being hired in anticipation of turnover even when no immediate opening existed. Those days are gone. The seller's market has metamorphosed into a buyer's market, and there has been a partial revival of the original concept that work permits should be granted only to those foreigners who offer special services not provided by burghers. But my experience is worth recounting because it is still applicable to younger seekers of business jobs.

While in Klosters on a skiing vacation during my fifty-second year, I telephoned a portfolio manager at Credit Suisse who had visited us for a month at the Crocker Bank in San Francisco and he introduced me to a personnel manager, who invited me to come in the next day. When I arrived, this official put cash on the table to pay for my train fare, and after fifteen minutes he introduced me to the head of the research department, who was sufficiently impressed by my then *fast fliessend* (nearly fluent) German to spend three hours with me. The following week he called to say that the bank was interested in employing me.

The rest was easy, though it took time: I had to send not only my résumé, but also college and university transcripts and the names of three references, which were thoroughly checked. Two months later I was invited to fly in business class to work with the U.S. research team for a week, for which I was paid one thousand Swiss francs and provided free accommodation, and at the end of which I was offered a contract. I accepted and a few days later, after hiking up Gemmipass in Berner Oberland and subsequently swimming in Lake Zürich, I flew back to the U.S. to await a work permit, which required a further two and a half months – largely, I suspect, because of the dilatoriness of the personnel department.

Whereas in the 1980s foreign teachers (especially of English) were also very welcome, now the Swiss (like many other Europeans) are producing fewer than two children per family, and there are too many teachers. In the canton of Bern, the *Gymnasium* has been reduced from four years to three, and many teachers have seen their status cut from full-time to part-time. In this environment, the welcome mat for foreign teachers has been emphatically withdrawn, ironically, at the same time that, especially in Zürich, a record number of the offspring of fecund foreigners is reaching school age. Thus, while it may be more socially useful to contribute to the development of young minds than to help enrich European millionaires even further, corporate jobs are far easier to come by than teaching positions. Although public school teachers earn quite competitive salaries here, a former teacher turned businessman who seeks to return to pedagogy is regarded with suspicion, in Switzerland as elsewhere, as a materialistic capitalist.

A word about language protocols. The large banks generally compromise with bilingual foreigners by accepting the use of High German as opposed to the local Swiss-German dialect – which, except in the French-influenced canton of Basel, will sound like a disease of the throat. If you speak no German, your coworkers will speak English to you, but you will be encouraged to learn at least High German. Smaller companies may prove less willing to speak High German, which is called *Schriftdeutsch* or 'written' German, rather than *Hochdeutsch*, for two reasons: the Swiss do not like to think of their dialects as *Plattdeutsch*, or 'Low' German, and the dialects themselves are largely oral rather than written. (The Swiss alphabet conspicuously does not include the German ß.) A barometer of your standing at the firm will be the continued willingness of your coworkers and, especially, superiors to speak English or High German with you. Make no mistake: regardless of how fluent they may be, they regard speaking any language other than the local dialect as a major concession, which must be earned. Thus if your colleagues suddenly insist upon conversing with you in the local dialect, your tenure is probably in jeopardy.

In general, you will be treated well, with deference and formal respect. Do not expect to be encouraged to call your superiors by their first names for at least six months; when in doubt, address everyone formally. At meetings, formal usage is common even among friends; at parties, informal usage is countenanced even with superiors but will not be carried over to the next business day.

But you will have no power. Swiss banks are autocratic, not democratic–participative. Your opinion will seldom be solicited about the suitability of a candidate for employment in your specialty, and you are unlikely to meet him or her before he or she begins work. You will not be able to have a voice in the distribution of commissions to brokers, for example; such matters are decided by general managers.

The autocratic nature of Swiss banks reflects the society as a whole. Approvals are required for quite mundane endeavors. For example, when Credit Suisse was preparing to move its research department to an old hotel, the Simplon, which it had purchased and refurbished, it built an air conditioning well adjacent to an appropriate window in each office, and then, when the building was ready for reoccupancy, the bank applied to the civic authorities for permission to install the machines in the wells. Permission was denied on the grounds that the building was a landmark. Unwilling to spend ten million Swiss francs to strengthen the roof sufficiently to support a giant water tank, the bank placed temperature charting devices in strategically located offices, took readings of thirty to thirty-five degrees Celsius (seventy-seven to eighty-six degrees Fahrenheit) for two summers and, armed with this evidence, reapplied. Permission was again denied. So, a couple of years later still, the bank abandoned the building and moved its employees elsewhere.

If you wish to take a business trip back to the United States, it will probably require the approval of a general manager, who will 'suggest' modifications to your schedule but who is otherwise likely to be supportive. Since it may take him a month to approve your trip, plan ahead. (Do not be surprised if you never actually meet him; in three years at Credit Suisse, I was never introduced to one and later, at a private bank, I never met any of the outside directors.)

Taking courses is encouraged. The Swiss love to take courses. My personnel officer at Credit Suisse took at least two per year. Often they are given in attractive mountain settings. One prominent annual series is sponsored by the Swiss Banking School. The catch, of course, is that they are almost invariably offered only in Swiss-German so the best way to take advantage of this perquisite, at least initially, is to ask for private language instruction, preferably at Berlitz. No matter how well you have kept up your college German, you will need both a refresher course in grammar and, especially, a new and extensive business vocabulary. When I arrived here ready for work, I remembered from German literature how to say 'objectivity' and 'song of fate' in German, but I did not know the words for 'asset management', 'debt', 'earnings', 'mortgage' or 'interest rate'. A two-week course of private lessons at Berlitz polished my grammar and added two thousand words commonly used in business to my German vocabulary. I missed, however, a rare opportunity to spend a couple of days learning the Zürich dialect of Swiss-German, although my accent is said to be Swiss rather than German.

Except for lunch, or occasional after-hours drinks, do not expect to socialize with your coworkers away from the office. It is customary for one to bring cakes or cookies on one's own birthday, to give an *apéro* upon promotion or when leaving the firm honorably, and occasionally to bring croissants or ice cream.

About office etiquette: although the Swiss are far from prudish, there will be no naked couples jumping out of cakes, male first, as occurred at Bear Stearns' San Francisco office in the mid-1980s on the occasion of a top executive's birthday, and it is only the American brokers like Cowen who fax their clients such things as *Spy* magazine's indecent cover 'photo' of Hillary Clinton wielding the whip on healthcare reform. One does not brandish the business end of a collapsed and compressed Knirps black umbrella at a female colleague and ask her what it reminds her of, as I once did to the delight of a black female professional coworker at Metropolitan Life Insurance Company in New York. A bond salesman does not accuse a female institutional bond trader of 'being the type who likes a lot of foreplay' because she has inquired about a new issue's coupon, yield to maturity and sinking fund provisions, as an amused Irish-American woman of that profession in San Francisco once recounted had just happened to her.[1]

Contrary to popular belief, the Swiss do have a sense of humor. For example, if you make fun of someone's 'Aquascrotum raincoat' or if you make a pun on the word for veal stew, *Kalbsvoressen*, by calling it *Kalbsnachessen*, or even if – like Steve Stahle, a memorable institutional salesman at Drexel's San Francisco office a decade ago – you refer to Shitake mushrooms as shitcake fungi, your colleagues will get the point and laugh.

But there are severe limits. Your coworkers, if they read at all, are still likely to share very few points of reference with you. Topical jokes like those told by my favorite comedian, Rock King of Cape Cod, will fall flat: e.g. vintage early 1980s, 'I will now play Edward Schlossberg's favorite song, *Nothing Could Be Finer*.' Even puns are not comprehended. At the private bank I worked for, in order to humor my boss's penchant for American comic books, I once appended to a report one of Rock's jokes as a caption to a *New Yorker* cartoon depicting a doctor conferring with a

---

[1]There are shenanigans reserved for wealthy clients, especially visiting Arab ones, for whom the large banks are rumored to spend hundreds of thousands of francs annually to procure prostitutes.

patient's husband: 'Your wife has acute angina.' 'How about that!' No non-native speaker of English in the entire office grasped the *double-entendre*.

Similarly, if you report that a Barnes and Noble salesman in New York, upon being asked to recommend a book for a colleague in the hospital, suggested William Faulkner's *As I Lay Dying*, you will elicit a chuckle; but if you announce that a new edition of Ernest Hemingway's *A Farewell to Arms* features a reproduction of the Venus de Milo on the cover, the blank stare you will probably receive indicates a total lack of conversance with the world of art.

Again, if you report that a television newscaster garbled the name of Karla Faye Tucker, the convicted pickaxe murderess recently executed in Texas, your coworkers will laugh – if they understand what 'garbled' means. But if you say that a fundamentalist institution of higher learning located in Tulsa, Oklahoma, and named after a famous television evangelist, is being renamed in honor of President Clinton, your pun will be lost upon your listeners.

While you will encounter colleagues at classical concerts, they tend to view the event as a social rather than cultural outing. Recently I mentioned to a portfolio manager in his late fifties that his given names, Franz Joseph, were the same as Haydn's. This came as news to him; he had only heard of the composer being referred to as Joseph Haydn. How he could have missed encountering the full name on compact discs or radio stations baffles me; I am reminded of a former female analyst from Met Life in New York whose surname is Villalobos, and who by her early forties had never heard of the composer of that name.

Of course, despite the cultural gap, you may eventually make some friends, even among those of the opposite sex. There is a surprising number of professional women working at the large banks, despite residual reluctance on the part of many supervisors to risk hiring someone who will probably get married and reproduce within a few years, and a lot of coupling goes on at the large banks, much of it leading to cohabitation and marriage.

But be careful: if romance blossoms, or lust awakens, use protection. You are in Europe, after all, that decadent continent where a lot of experimentation, casual affairs and sexual exploitation occur, and where the Biblical injunction to 'love thy neighbor' easily takes precedence over the Seventh and Tenth Commandments and the proscriptions in Leviticus. Here, as elsewhere, the sentiment 'When I'm not with the girl I love, I love the girl I'm with' is equally true for many members of both sexes. Indeed, Switzerland has one of the highest rates of AIDS in Europe, particularly in Zürich, because the city fathers in their infinite wisdom decided that the best way to inhibit the spread of the drug culture was to outlaw the over-the-counter sale of hypodermic needles. As a result, of course, addicts shared needles and AIDS proliferated. Three years ago, moreover, Swiss voters approved a referendum reducing the age of consensual sex between minors from sixteen to fourteen! Clearly, children here quickly grow up into adultery.

At least in the beginning, however, you should expect to be on your own when you leave the office (unless, of course, you have a spouse). Many of your colleagues will have access to their parents' or friends' cottages in the mountains and they invariably repair there on weekends, and seldom if ever go anywhere else. Do not expect to be invited for dinner or as a house guest, or even to join them in a social activity should you happen to meet them away from the office. They are unlikely to introduce you to their spouses or close friends, let alone to an eligible single person of the opposite sex. But your offsetting advantage is that you can sample a wide range of skiing and hiking areas, notwithstanding the fact that season passes are the most economical option. Indeed, you are likely to experience more of Switzerland than most of its burghers.

If you work for a private Swiss bank, your isolation is likely to be even greater. It may sound tautological, but private bankers are intensely private individuals, usually wealthy and invariably eager to increase the distance between you and them. (In this book I have respected their desire for privacy by not naming directly any of my professional acquaintance.) If you meet one on a ski lift, he is undoubtedly with an instructor who is leading his party somewhere you can't go, perhaps (in bad weather) off-piste through the woods along a route that you are clearly not welcome to follow. He will point out his wide powder skis (made by *Völkl*), which he bought in Canada, erroneously inform you that they are not yet available in Switzerland and talk about running into Prince Charles wearing the same type of loden coat as himself.

At the private bank I worked for, there was a noticeable degree of monasticism. Except in the legal department, the sexes never went to lunch together; once, by coincidence, a number of female assistants encountered a similar number of male portfolio managers at a restaurant. Greetings were exchanged, but the two groups were seated at separate tables, and by and large they ignored each other. I happened to be eating there with a friend from another private bank and he remarked on the anomaly. Similarly, at the nearby swimming facility on the lake, male and female employees regularly ignored each other. Whenever I encountered a female assistant at a concert she was invariably accompanied by a female colleague. On the tram home, several coworkers were usually present, but they almost never spoke to one another. I violated this taboo with glee, ostentatiously escorting the chairman's secretary to lunch on a couple of occasions and once to dinner, but few followed my example.

The bank sponsored two events per year for employees: a Christmas dinner at a fancy restaurant – the Dolder Hotel's dining room, for example – and a cultural or recreational outing in summer. A trip to the Jungfrau restaurant one year was followed by a private performance, sponsored by the bank, of Dvorak's opera *The Rusalka*. Clients, honored guests and employees filled the entire opera house.

Less than three weeks before my scheduled starting date, the summer gala was held at a director's wine chateau on Lac Léman, the lake of Geneva. I was not invited, although it would have been an ideal way to introduce a new employee to his colleagues.

(My revenge, however unintended, was realized when the host, an aging Teutonic multimillionaire whose lust to increase his fortune constituted classic Freudian anal eroticism, purchased per my unfortunate recommendation the excessive number of three thousand shares of U.S. Surgical at sixty-five dollars. The shares, which had fallen from one hundred and thirty-five dollars when Johnson & Johnson announced its entry into the laparoscopic or microsurgical instrument market, recovered to seventy-eight dollars, but the gentleman had misplaced his faith in my target price of ninety dollars and held on. The stock, as you may remember, plummeted below twenty dollars – half of Dan Dorfman's prediction, when it was in the mid-50s, that it would sink below forty dollars. The vintner unloaded at thirty-five dollars, suffering a loss, including commissions, of nearly one hundred thousand dollars on an investment in – ironically, and, I am sure, unwittingly – an essentially Jewish firm.)

At the semiannual events, as well as at occasional after-work parties on the bank's premises to bid farewell to retiring or otherwise honorably departing colleagues, the foreigners among us gathered together on the periphery of the crowd. Even those who spoke fluent Swiss-German and had acquired Swiss spouses were largely ignored by the mainstream guests. You can live in Switzerland for twenty years, but you will only be tolerated, never embraced or fully accepted. Once per decade the Swiss hold a referendum on expelling all 'guest workers' who, they feel, are depriving citizens of jobs. The politicians assiduously remind the Swiss of all the dirty jobs unworthy of Swiss citizens that are performed by foreigners and the measure fails, but the sentiment in favor of this form of ethnic cleansing lingers on. Periodic attempts to permit foreigners a limited voting franchise also invariably fail.

Because the Swiss never forget that you are an invited guest, neither should you. Always defer to them; allow them to go ahead of you in queues (known as *Schlangen*, or 'snakes', in German); be humble in conversation. This is impossible to do all of the time, but you should try not to portray the 'ugly American' more than twice per year. Remember, although you may think of yourself as an expatriate, the Swiss will always regard you as an immigrant, present on sufferance and presumption of good behavior. And the native ability to understand English seems to improve dramatically whenever you curse at them.

Should you become obviously unemployed, the hostile attitude will harden: the Swiss understandably resent paying taxes to provide unemployment compensation for foreigners and especially during recessions they would prefer that you leave the country permanently rather than compete with their countrymen for a job.

Yes, there is a Swiss-American club, but I can't recommend it. Most of the Americans you will meet there are transient dental hygienists and the like who plan to spend a year here before moving on to, say, Australia. You are unlikely to meet an American who has roots here, as he or she generally has a Swiss parent or spouse and avoids gatherings of the parvenus. Nearly all of the Swiss who show up are attracted only by the free drinks; they generally have serious attachments elsewhere who do not accompany them to such events.

Two far better alternatives are the Swiss chapter of the Association for Investment Management and Research, and the British-Swiss Chamber of Commerce. The former has only about one hundred members, but they are among the cream of Swiss investment professionals; some of them earned MBAs at Harvard, Wharton or Fletcher, though rarely Stanford, and they are intelligent, articulate, multilingual and internationalist or even cosmopolitan rather than provincial in outlook. The latter features distinguished guest speakers who are generally not investment professionals but rather politicians, economists, lawyers or doctors, and attracts a commensurately accomplished clientele. Both organizations charge annual dues of one hundred and twenty Swiss francs and luncheon fees ranging from forty to seventy Swiss francs.

If you work for an American firm, your salary and social opportunities are likely to be better than at a Swiss firm. You will probably receive health insurance, which is subsidized by only the largest Swiss firms, as well as a housing allowance, which is unknown among the Swiss. But there will be some prudishness as well. A female employee shocked her colleagues at IBM by appearing topless at a company swimfest – notwithstanding that most of them have wives or girlfriends who, like many Swiss women, go topless at lakeside swimming facilities.

No equivalent of the United Fund exists in Switzerland and the only office collections are to fund presents for retiring or departing coworkers. Charity is entirely a private matter here. You will receive solicitations by post, often accompanied by unsolicited folding cards and envelopes. There are biannual clothing drives, with marked plastic bags deposited in your mailbox. You can deduct five hundred Swiss francs from your annual Swiss taxes for charitable gifts without documentation. Swiss institutional charity does not extend to the illegitimate children of foreign workers, who must marry before their children are permitted to enroll in a public school.

A word about Swiss taxes. There are three sorts which are mandatory: direct federal taxes, or *Bundesteuer*; taxes for the canton and neighborhood, or *Germeindesteuer*; and income taxes, or *Quellensteuer*. In Zürich, the last two types are based, after the first year, on the prior year's income; in Basel, on the current year's. The large banks provide local tax services for a fee, and I recommend employing them, at least initially. Once you have a 'C' permit, no payroll deductions will be made for income taxes and you will have to learn to save for them, as do the Swiss, so that you can pay them not quarterly, but at the end of the year. Combined, Swiss taxes account for roughly twenty-one percent of gross salary. If you leave Switzerland before normal retirement age, your entire pension account, including your monthly after-tax contributions, will be subject to an additional tax of six and a half percent which will be withheld before the funds are unfrozen and released to you.

I used the word 'mandatory' advisedly, because there is a fourth kind of tax which is, in effect, optional: the religious tax. When you apply for your first visa or work permit, you will be asked to state your *Konfession*, or religion. If you answer Catholic or Protestant, you will be liable for a small tax to support that church. If you reply in any other way – Buddhist, Shinto, no religion – you will not be liable for this tax. Thus many Swiss as well as foreigners indicate for this purpose that they practice no religion.

(The same question appears on employment and rental applications and you can simply leave it blank, as I invariably have done. No one will challenge you on this matter.)

There is also a small (0.25%) tax on capital which many holders of Swiss bank accounts avoid by taking shelter under the banking secrecy laws, i.e. by not declaring such accounts. There is no tax on capital gains, of course, and most European countries – especially the Scandinavian ones – have significantly higher taxes on capital. Since charges made to Swiss Mastercards and Visa cards are deducted from the related bank account at the end of the month, the phenomenon of such credit organizations advertising annual percentage rates of 'only' 15.3% is largely unknown here.

You must continue to file U.S. returns as well, even though you are unlikely to owe any actual tax, in order to avoid difficulties when you repatriate, or even when passing through U.S. Customs on return visits. Generally, the combination of excess housing allowance, earned income exemption and foreign tax credit will enable you to avoid U.S. taxes. By 30th June of each year you must also file a disclosure of your foreign bank accounts with the U.S. Treasury. During your first year, the U.S. Embassy in Bern will provide necessary forms, and you should telephone it each year to request a breakdown of the official annual and monthly exchange rates between the U.S. dollar and the Swiss franc. In subsequent years, the IRS will send you a packet containing both the customary forms and the special ones for expatriates.

A word about pension accounts. Most private employers offer one and require participation either from your first day at work or retroactively from the age of twenty-five. In the latter case, your employer will usually help you buy in the back years through a combination grant and interest-bearing loan. If you are older, the level of participation for the back years may be reduced to as low as forty percent from the standard seventy percent. Ongoing contributions (about seven percent of gross salary) are deducted from monthly take-home pay (which is deposited directly to your account rather than transacted by check). You cannot withdraw pension funds, and borrowing is limited in amount and can generally be only for the purpose of financing the purchase of a house or apartment. Since any money paid in before the age of twenty-five does not count toward an eventual pension, most Swiss who begin to work at an earlier age resign about six months before turning twenty-five, declare *Selbständigkeit* or financial self-reliance and thus recapture the funds, then return to work soon after attaining the age of twenty-five. In the event of retirement – voluntary or not – before becoming eligible for a private pension, one can gain access to the accumulated funds by making a similar declaration; permission is required for foreigners.

Let me return to the customary thrift of the Swiss. You have undoubtedly heard of the secrecy mandated by Swiss banking laws so you will be surprised, as I was, to learn that – at least at the private bank I worked for – all investment accounts on the books there were open to my scrutiny, and to that of many other employees, the rationale being that in this way analysts and portfolio managers could compare their recommendations and holdings with those of their colleagues. It was no shock to learn that the top officers are wealthy, with the chairman's investment account fluctuating between twelve million and fourteen million Swiss francs; or that the general manager's annual bonus was at least two hundred thousand Swiss francs which, according to the computer, he had deposited at the Geneva branch of a large bank; or even that the bright and bearded Swiss analyst in the next office – whose clothes were shabby and smelly and whose shoes, by his own account, never cost as much as two hundred Swiss francs – had accumulated over six hundred thousand Swiss francs. But I was impressed to learn that my secretary – an unusually literate if casual woman who wore blue jeans and muslin blouses, who often ate lunch at her desk while reading such inspirational tomes as Nicholas Katzenbach's *The Wisdom of Teams*, and whose Greek husband was and may still be an unemployed disc jockey – had saved upwards of two hundred thousand Swiss francs. No wonder the Swiss are so rail-thin! They eat little, yet almost invariably they brush their teeth in the unisex office bathrooms after a lunch as light as an apple.

Chapter III
Swiss Banking Practices
Affecting the Consumer

Because most employees of Swiss banks are relatively young and inexperienced, errors are frequent and the customer usually pays. For example, I once deposited a Merrill Lynch Ready Assets check from the U.S. at a regional branch of Credit Suisse, which sent it to the main office in Zürich, which forwarded it to Credit Suisse in New York, which mailed it to Bankers Trust in New York, which dispatched it to the Florida bank upon which it was written. Somewhere along the way, a diagonal line appeared across the numeral '8', making it look as though someone had tried to change it to a '9'. This caused the check to be dishonored, which at first was reported as lost. After six weeks, I received a photocopy of the check; after four months, the original. I eventually had to pay expenses of one hundred and thirteen Swiss francs for attempting to deposit this check in my Swiss bank account, and the check itself had to be replaced, even though the amount written in words (which, rather than the numerical expression, is legally binding in the U.S.) had not been tampered with.

This experience points up the fact that Swiss banks do not like to handle foreign personal checks. There are no personal checks in Switzerland: one pays bills by carrying cash to the post office, or by filling out a payment order at the bank teller or (if one has a postal account) post office window. There are bank drafts, a type of certified check known as 'cross checks', which must be deposited to one's account rather than cashed directly, as well as Eurochecks, which are tied to a debit card and are honored by many stores and gasoline stations, but no one mails a personal check anywhere. For recurrent fixed expenses, such as rent, a standing order is invariably used. The debit cards can also be used directly in many stores and hotels.

The postal accounts are used by many Swiss to collect incoming funds (e.g. from tenants) before transferring them to their bank accounts. This arrangement preserves the secret of one's bank affiliation from his debtors, and facilitates the paying of bills at post office windows.

In an ironic twist, the commercial banks are now encouraging depositors to direct incoming funds to the *banks' post office accounts* rather than to the depositors' own bank accounts, and they are providing forms to facilitate this, touting the convenience to the customers' debtors. The banks' real purpose, of course, is to capture the interest on the funds during the several days they require to transfer the money to the individual accounts designated on the forms. They also lower costs by causing postal clerks rather than bank tellers to book the transactions. Finally, since postal transactions are comparatively transparent to the Swiss authorities, the banks may well be promoting their use as a means of fulfilling their responsibility to avoid becoming a conduit for moneys flowing from illegal activities.

If you have an American Express card, it is a good idea to keep it, using the U.S. address of a friend or relative. This should not jeopardize your tax status as a foreign resident, but it will reduce the annual subscription cost (currently fifty-five dollars in the U.S. and one hundred and forty Swiss francs in Switzerland) and preserve your U.S. credit rating for your eventual repatriation. You should also maintain one U.S. Visa or Mastercard. When you need to pay these bills in dollars, the simplest way is to visit an American Express office. Your American Express bill can be paid there in either dollars or francs, and for the other bills you can buy money orders on the spot for eight Swiss francs, or fifteen Swiss francs to thirty Swiss francs and a day's delay at the branch of your Swiss bank where you opened your account, or fifty Swiss francs and a longer delay at another branch. A Swiss bank at which you have no account will simply refuse to sell you a money order or bank cheque denominated in U.S. dollars!

At the same time, you should apply for a local Visa or Mastercard, so that your European charges can be directly deducted at the month's end from your Swiss bank account. Although the Swiss have come to accept and even to embrace the use of credit cards, not all establishments accept them and there is still a prevailing sentiment that if you use credit you must have no money. The Swiss do not understand, let alone like or welcome, people without money. Germans and English tourists often bring ten thousand Swiss francs in cash on their vacations, and even though many banks post signs warning against carrying large amounts of cash, it remains a common practice.

Admittedly, there may be months when a Visa or Mastercard deduction is made from your bank account without a preceding statement from the card issuer. If you call and ask, you may be promised a statement, which doesn't come, or you may be told, more truthfully, that the person responsible for mailing statements is away from the office. You will have to wait until he or she returns; no one else can or will fulfill your request. If you are lucky, someone may read the month's charges to you.

At Credit Suisse, telephones in the research department were simply not answered between noon and 2 p.m., as it was assumed that callers would realize that it was lunchtime. While an analyst could transfer his calls to the unit secretary's telephone, that too was unlikely to be answered during these hours.

Expect small charges on your monthly bank statement for depositing business checks or U.S. dollar-denominated traveler's checks, ordering bank checks and purchasing traveler's checks denominated in non-Swiss currencies. Statements are invariably mailed in plain envelopes bearing no return address lest your mail carrier discover which bank you patronize – a violation of banking secrecy laws! Unless you specify and agree to pay for first-class mail, most banks now routinely send all mail (including responses to employment inquiries) second class, which takes three business days instead of one, in order to save twenty centimes per letter.

If you choose to have a numbered account, rather than one in your own or a nominee's name, you will not be able to access it with a debit card bearing a PIN code.

Some 'light' was shed on the question of how Swiss banks work out interest on deposits by a recent offer sent me by my health insurer offering a two percent discount if I paid annually rather than quarterly: this discount, the offer averred, was equivalent to a four and a half percent annual interest rate! The same offer noted that a way to mitigate rising premiums on the basic (and obligatory) coverage was to increase the annual 'franchise' or deductible amount, assuring me that the savings in premiums normally more than offset the higher deductible. Then followed the specifics: if I increased the annual deductible from three hundred Swiss francs to six hundred Swiss francs, my monthly premium for basic insurance in 1997 would decline from SwFr 172.10 to SwFr 152.90. Similar Swiss 'arithmetic' can apply to special holiday discount combinations offered by the Swiss railways. *Caveat emptor.*

When you leave Switzerland and notify your bank to mail monthly statements to a U.S. address, subtle changes in attitude become apparent. The withholding of thirty-five percent of earned interest for three years becomes permanent. You are encouraged to surrender all credit and debit cards on the ground that they will not be useful overseas. If you insist on keeping any of the cards which permit you to withdraw cash from other banks' teller machines or to charge purchases, a substantial sum may be frozen to guarantee payment. Suddenly your own bank's teller machine automatically interrogates you in English, rather than in German, and it no longer offers you a choice of tongues. Bank statements mailed to the U.S. also employ English. Anyone who owes you money will, upon learning of your repatriation, balk at paying it; any person or institution to which you owe money will press you for immediate repayment. The Swiss project their own cavalier attitude toward debts outside the country to foreigners returning home, and any Swiss to whom you owe nothing will advise you to forget about repaying your debts once you leave. Honesty is clearly relative under such circumstances.

Chapter IV
Investing Through a Swiss Bank

As my unfortunate experience (described at the beginning of the preceding chapter) in depositing a personal check suggests, there is a high degree of incompetence at the large Swiss banks, which this chapter attempts to document with a view toward helping you answer this question: Do you really want your investments managed by a thirty year old Swissie with no university education? Do you really wish to grant a mandate, i.e. full discretion, to a Swiss bank?

When I first reported for work at Credit Suisse, I was struck by an apparition straight out of *A Brave New World*: the scotch-taping of computer-generated line graphs on the walls next to the office across the corridor from mine. Inside this office were hundreds more; indeed, the graphs first filled the available wall-space in this office and only then spilled onto the walls outside it.

Of what did these graphs consist? The product of two (subsequently three) full-time employees, the chief of whom was a vice-president named Bertschi, they charted Elliott Waves in the market and in life. I do not pretend to understand this arcane discipline, and I was not helped by the highly derivative monthly newsletters published in poor English by the unit, but the basic concept is that most uptrends lead to a correction of exactly sixty-two and a half percent, or five-eighths, of the previous advance. The most interesting of these graphs depicted the Venus de Milo, whose waist is five-eighths of her bust and hip measurements, and who thus validates the Elliott Wave theory!

A few years ago, when the Dow Jones Industrial Average was around five thousand, one of the technical models run by this unit predicted that it would fall to about twelve hundred. During a lengthy telephone interview with *The Wall Street Journal*, I happened to mention this and of course that startling prediction – attributed to me by name – proved to be the only sound bite which the newspaper chose to print. Thenceforth, Credit Suisse informed the paper that only Claude Zwick, one of its senior trading executives, was authorized to discuss the bank's stock market outlook.

When I imprudently mentioned my surprise at the existence of the Elliott Wave unit to the head of the research department, he smiled and said that he thought that part of the department's efforts should consist of 'pure' (rather than applied) research in the scientific sense, à la Ciba-Geigy. The analogy proved pregnant, as you will see.

In this spirit, we developed two small subdepartments, each headed by a vice-president with a doctorate from the University of London, and devoted to what became known as financial analytics. These individuals, a Finnish male and a Philippine female who lived together and had been hired as a team, went out and gave erudite lectures on bond trading – complete with abstruse mathematical formulas and charts – to the regional portfolio managers, who rarely if ever understood them. The objective, of course, as proudly explained by the department head, was to encourage active trading so that the bank could capture not only more commissions but also a small spread (between the bid and asked prices in a negotiated market) on each trade.

These departments were shunted around from research to treasury to trading, and eventually the male guru was dismissed for trying to grab too much power.

The U.S. research unit for which I worked was comprised of a supervisor, a secretary and six analysts, three of them neophytes. The supervisor, a Swiss (naturally) by the name of Bruno Guldener, is a male chauvinist whose reflexive comment upon seeing my rubber overshoes, which are unknown in Switzerland, was that he had a wife to clean his boots. (Like other Swiss wives with children, she can look forward to making lunch at least twice per school day until their children enter the Gymnasium, or university preparatory school. In all of Zürich, there are only three all-day schools below this level.) Bruno is also a born-again quantitative analyst who discovered this approach after failing as a fundamental analyst. To make the distinction simply, he focused on the past rather than on the future despite the fact that the market is always attempting to discount the perceived future efficiently.

Bruno's system, which he derived largely from Salomon Brothers, Goldman Sachs and Donaldson, Lufkin and Jenrette, emphasized a combination of cash inflows and outflows, volume and price, in attempting to predict short-term trading moves. It was analogous to the Bridge Data approach, which attempts to identify support and resistance levels by similar analysis of these three factors. But while no one pretends that the Bridge system is all-inclusive, precluding other types of research, Bruno believed with the fervor of the newly converted that he had devised an exclusive lock on investment truth. Other quantitative 'systems' such as those of Value Line or Columbine which attempt to rank stocks' next twelve months' relative performance potential based on comparative price and earnings momentum are also highly popular among Swiss investment professionals.

To implement his approach, Bruno had developed a long macro in six segments, each of which took three and a half hours to execute, and which he therefore required all of us except the secretary to run each Monday morning, thus effectively tying up our computers until lunchtime. The output was a simple buy, hold or sell advice for each of the several hundred stocks in our database, and it was widely ignored by portfolio managers.

At the same time, Bruno put the neophytes to work charting indicators and economic series in a search for ways to predict interim movements of the U.S. market – what he called 'correlations'. His charges did not learn security analysis, accounting, economics, etc., they merely plotted charts all day long, like traders who never trade.

But they were assigned industries, their areas of responsibility were widely disseminated, and they were expected to publish analyses of company earnings and events and to make buy, hold, or sell recommendations. Also, portfolio managers from various branches would often call with a request for an instant opinion on a stock in which clients then present in their office were interested.

What to do? Most of these 'analysts' had arrived believing that 'following' stocks meant watching the electronic ticker tape record trades all day long – an attitude I had last encountered in the 1970s in New York at the long-since defunct firm of F.I. DuPont. Most of them possessed neither an innate sense of value nor a yardstick for determining if a stock was cheap or expensive, so they resorted to measuring price-earnings ratios both absolutely and relative to the market, along with price-book value ratios, dividend yields and the like.

I showed them how to measure a stock's risk and reward based on the relationship between its current relative price-earnings ratio and the ten-year average high and low ratios, and they gratefully ran this program every day, using its results not, as I intended, to display anomalies in valuations relative to industries or the market which invited further research, but as a definitive answer. They could say to a portfolio manager that, based on the ten-year norm, the stock in question had negative risk and was thus deeply undervalued; the manager would attempt to repeat this to the client, thus endorsing the latter's inclination to purchase said stock, and the transaction was made. No attention was paid to such fundamental factors as the issuer's financial condition, operating leverage, inflation sensitivity, competitive position, technological superiority or inferiority, quality of management, historical returns or takeover potential.

It goes without saying that these so-called analysts never read annual reports, trade publications or business magazines, although they did read *The Wall Street Journal* and brokers' reports, and they had access to various computerized news retrieval services, including those published by Dow Jones and Reuters. With these tools they attempted to perform secondary research on U.S. equities. When they attended presentations, they did ample justice to the freshly squeezed blood orange juice, fine foods and wines, but – like their counterparts from other institutions – they seldom asked a question, and never an intelligent one. I even doubt that they understood the concept that gains in the stock market are contingent upon improvement in the bond market, which is a strategist's typical way of saying that interest rates must fall in order for price-earnings ratios to expand.

Their inferiority to U.S. analysts was underscored when I attended a Morgan Stanley aerospace-defense conference in New York in early 1993. During the question-and-answer period, I asked Raytheon's chairman whether his company was developing a defense against incoming strategic missiles, and he replied in the affirmative. Later, a young analyst attending the conference showed me the relevant section in Raytheon's annual report. Such conscientiousness simply does not exist in Switzerland.

Once, William Smithburg, the chief executive officer of Quaker Oats, aware that his company's shares were significantly owned in accounts managed by Credit Suisse, decided at a late moment to accompany his female director of investor relations to a meeting with Raymond Frech, our worst analyst, who happened to have been assigned the food industry, and the feedback from Mr. Smithburg was understandably unfavorable. Upon hearing this, I asked our analyst for his impressions of the meeting, and he answered that it went smoothly, and that I should have met the stunning woman accompanying her boss!

A brief postscript: when our department was dissolved, this analyst was transferred to one of the private banks owned by Credit Suisse where his attempt to become a portfolio manager failed within six months. Yet he then went on first to a German bank, and then to Merrill Lynch, in exactly the same capacity, and today he travels to Germany to advise clients on their holdings! Since *frech* means 'bold' in German, I have nicknamed him Raymond the Bold.

In a similar vein, I must tell you about Monica, a short but vivacious young woman with sparkling brown eyes who comes from Montreal, where her Swiss father and Canadian mother (from whom she derives dual citizenship) own a jewelry store. Hired reluctantly by Bruno Guldener[1] after I pressed him to add a woman to our all-male team, Monica quickly learned the vocabulary of investing, but not the concepts; from beneath her ponytail there emerged about what you would expect from such a place. An

---

[1]Tellingly, Bruno, who spoke excellent English, invariably insisted upon referring to Monica in her absence as 'he'.

inexhaustible talker in both English and the Zürich dialect (learned from her Swiss father), she soon informed me that her salary (still being paid by the personnel department rather than the investment department) should be as high as mine because she did the same work. The head of the department, Dr. Peter Dellsperger, admired her spunk, and tolerated her naive complaints. Behind his back, she called him Dr. Dumbburger. If Monica were a man, she would have lots of Sertoli cells. Being a woman, she will doubtless marry someone named Klein Hoden. (I won't explain this; if your German doesn't include either or both of these words, you'll have to consult a German-English dictionary.)

Monica was and remains a chain smoker. Since the rest of us were, thankfully, all non-smokers, she would go outside the office to smoke, but then stand in the doorway and talk to us while the draft filled the room with her exhaust. A novice skier, she would attempt to invite herself to join me on skiing vacations, thinking that it would be fun. 'For whom?' I once asked, only to be accused of insensitivity.

When our unit was terminated – although she could have stayed on for several years as an analyst covering the Canadian market, which continued to be followed by the research department in Zürich – Monica eschewed my suggestion of applying to the private bank where she had an account, on the grounds that as a junior analyst she would not be able to attend many presentations. Monica loved presentations, not so much for the elegant hotel fare as for the captive audience of men seated around her. Instead, she found a more senior job at another prestigious private bank, Coutts.

I competed for this position, as I had for the one my assistant won, was refused, complained that they were biased against age and experience, and received a reply assuring me that they sought to hire only persons 'with profound experience'. Then they hired Monica. She lasted six months, and at the time of writing has been unemployed for the past eight months. When I learned this, I again sought a position with Coutts, and was once again turned down because of age. The pupil thrives, the teacher languishes: such is business, music and life. Barton Biggs of Morgan Stanley avers that most portfolio managers are between twenty-eight and thirty-eight years of age. None of them, accordingly, has experienced a recession, stagflation, a bear market, or a market stuck in a trading range.

Upon encountering acquaintances at the unemployment office, Monica was not embarrassed to acknowledge – in front of any and all present, many of whom understand spoken English – that she continued to manage her family's substantial account at the highly regarded private bank to which she still refused to apply for a position. Nor did she display any qualms about showing off her Patek Philippe wristwatch, which she boasted was worth twenty-five thousand Canadian dollars. She also mentioned a standing offer to work as a broker for a major firm's office in Lugano.

Clearly, Monica was enjoying a long, lightly paid vacation, courtesy of the Swiss taxpayer. During this time, she changed apartments often and at one point had *two*, one for entertaining guests and one for 'studying'. Then she disappeared. An acquaintance at a French bank told me that she had 'flipped', which was about as much news as learning that former President Reagan had contracted Alzheimer's disease. I suspect that she returned to Montreal, Daddy, jewelry and eligible men, none of whom – unlike a Swiss boyfriend she once complained of – would expect her to wash his underwear on weekend trips together.

You may wonder what Bruno was doing all this time. Well may you ask. Bruno sat in his office with the door closed, extending his 'system' to other markets in preparation for a bid to become deputy head of the department, a position held then and now by the head of the team of analysts conducting primary research on the Swiss market. The advantage of this lack of supervision was, for me, a total absence of pressure to perform the busy work required of the others and freedom to recommend stocks in a timely fashion without seeking anyone's approval – no committees to cajole, no directors to inform, entertain, or anticipate off-the-wall questions from; no demands to track down a traveling brokerage analyst whose influence on market behavior had long since ebbed. After a year, my reputation was good enough that Bruno officially conceded I was no longer expected to perform 'quantitative' research. In turn, I submitted to a one hour explanation of his 'system', and I held my peace when he noted on my annual review that I showed little interest in this type of analysis. Bruno's management style confirmed my long-held impression that most research directors are about as useful as a conductor at a concert of chamber music.

One morning, Bruno invited me to have lunch with him and two visiting firemen from a new Credit Suisse affiliate, the recently purchased BEA Securities in New York. BEA, whose excellent reputation rests on sophisticated quantitative methods of investing, primarily in bonds, uses derivatives widely, and, although one of the visitors, a salesman, admitted that the firm's record of preserving investors' capital during synchronized worldwide bear markets was shaky, the firm had been highly successful in attracting and retaining clients, and it was quite profitable. Eventually, it took over First Boston's capital management operations as well as those of the far less successful Credit Suisse Asset Management organization in New York, which relied on a cumbersome committee approach and required its researchers to analyze brokerage reports exhaustively; its chairman, Kenneth J. Tarr, apparently did not recognize that by the time a broker recommends a stock it is seldom the optimal time to invest in it.

In contrast, BEA's chief executive officer, William Priest, is a successful businessman, erudite intellectual and serious art collector who loves young people, staffs his firm with them – including some from Credit Suisse in Zürich – and often invites them to dinner. Instead of seeking to learn from this paragon, Bruno, who had forced his way into BEA's offices on a recent trip to New York by invoking the authority of a general manager, expounded upon his system – or, rather, obsession. When he noted that he gave no weight to estimates and projections of future earnings and dividends, Bill Priest rolled his eyes and thought, no doubt, of the generous buyout of the remaining equity in his firm scheduled to occur some thirty months hence. I've always wished I could have told him about Bruno's musical taste, which ran to heavy metal.

All of us, including Bruno, landed on our feet when the department folded. Bruno spent two years in a portfolio management section trying to manage money with his model. The results were abysmal but in the process he learned about money management, and he took this experience with him to Union Bank of Switzerland, where today he is the chief portfolio manager and clients' tax preparer at the Zollikon branch. The best of the six, an American, actually transferred to a portfolio group six months before the rest of us had to scramble for a new job; we accused him – half seriously – of having possessed inside information. (Today, he works at a private bank.) Another of us joined a similar section; the youngest became a trader at the investment subsidiary of a large accounting firm. And, as adumbrated previously, I joined a private bank.

My own 'clients' at Credit Suisse, of course, were the portfolio managers whom we served. A typical caller would introduce himself, identify his branch or department, and then say, in dialect, 'Ich habe eine Frage,' (I have a question). In Swiss-German, this is rendered phonetically as 'Ee han uh frog', and it would invariably create in my mind an image of a manager with a telephone in one hand and a speaking frog, to whom he was about to introduce me, in the other. Often he would want no more than a Standard & Poors' tear sheet or, sometimes, a price chart, which I would create on the computer and send him by fax.

Nonetheless, I found these managers surprisingly risk-tolerant. Many invested actively for their own accounts as well as those of clients. At the end of 1991, I received a Christmas card hailing me as 'analyst of the year' from the branch in Zofingen, near Bern, along with a decent bottle of red wine (white wine is rarely chosen for a gift here). This resulted largely from my successful recommendation of a risk arbitrage situation, the Georgia Pacific-Great Northern Nekoosa merger, which was widely acted upon throughout the Credit Suisse organization, with purchases of call options exceeding those of shares of the target company. (I was also lucky, basing my recommendation on the relentless determination reflected in the acquirer's press releases, rather than on any inkling that the company would recognize and resolve the main anti-trust issue involved by arranging a quick sale of its safety paper division in Connecticut.)

When, inevitably, I later 'bagged' the managers with a poor recommendation – Community Psychiatric, whose chief competitor, National Medical Enterprises, brought regulators' wrath upon the entire industry by its alleged practice of paying bounty hunters to kidnap sundry individuals and commit them to its mental hospitals against their will – they showed sophistication and understanding.

Indeed, far from being composed of stuffy conservatives, the Zürich investment community is too tolerant of risk and extremely naive. Its members accept dubious claims of patent protection, such as those made by a British company called Asia Pacific Technology which has developed a system to extend the shelf life of fresh produce by treating it with nitrogen gas and covering it with saran wrap, or those made by a firm which cleans pipes with chemicals and claims a patent on a basic concept that is so all-encompassing as allegedly to require payment of royalties by anyone using any other chemical process for this purpose.

Virtually any Canadian shell company in the mining industry whose shares or warrants are listed on the highly disreputable Vancouver Stock Exchange can raise a few million dollars here, reflecting the affinity between Switzerland and Canada discussed later in this chapter. When pinstriped British brokers (including a member of the Palmer-Tomkinson family who socialize with the royals) come to town touting natural resources funds by promoting visions of five hundred dollar per ounce gold, the gnomes eagerly snap up the offerings. And even Nolan Bushnell (who founded Atari and subsequently opened a restaurant in Sunnyvale, California) was able to raise five million dollars for an unpatented peripheral device which he expected to be able to market for only six months before the majors came in and squeezed him out of the business. One suspects that the wealthy Swiss actually enjoy being financially raped from time to time; they certainly laughed heartily when former Cowen strategist Richard Hoffman entertained them at a symposium by recounting instances of their poor judgment.

Do not misinterpret this mild praise of the portfolio managers as a recommendation to open a fully discretionary or 'mandate' account at Credit Suisse. According to my former assistant there, who became a portfolio manager after working for the bank's New York affiliates for eighteen months and who is now employed as a U.S. analyst at a respected private bank, it was the policy and practice of Credit Suisse to sell any asset in a mandated account which had appreciated by ten percent. Since, at the time, the client's round trip commission typically cost five and two-tenths percent – although rates have subsequently declined somewhat, there are very few discount brokers in Switzerland – the bank got the lion's portion of this transaction: the round trip commissions accrued to its brokerage unit, and the Zürich stock exchange rebated to the bank a portion of all commissions on trades which it authorized to be executed there. Such rebates are, of course, neither passed on, in full or in part, nor even disclosed to the client, and they are illegal in the U.S. But in Switzerland they can comprise a significant portion of a bank's profits, which, in turn, are reflected in year-end bonuses.

In 1996, the regional stock exchanges merged, established their headquarters in Zürich, and the local exchange became known as the *Schweizer Börse*, or Swiss Exchange. While a number of U.S. companies (e.g. Pfizer) list their shares on foreign exchanges in recognition of widespread overseas ownership, the reverse is also true: companies wishing to establish or to broaden foreign distribution of their shares can facilitate the process by listing them abroad. Moreover, at least in Switzerland, the rebate system described in the preceding paragraph has proven to be a powerful incentive for investment managers to include in their clients' portfolios a representation of U.S. securities that are listed here. They clearly prefer to trade such shares on the Swiss Exchange than on the New York Stock Exchange, and often the entire portion of a geographically diversified portfolio allocated to American assets consists of U.S. shares that are so traded.

I once approached the head of the North American portfolio management department, a Mr. Scheller, about transferring to his department, and received this reply: 'Mr. Glueck, most of our U.S. clients are hiding assets from the IRS and we simply cannot communicate with them through another American.'

Indeed, my own experience bears this out. Two examples will suffice. I know one American living here who simply failed to file U.S. tax returns for five years, until the death of a parent released his inheritance and forced him to file for that year; I have no idea whether or how he explained the reporting hiatus. And while skiing in Zermatt recently, I encountered at the Olympia Stübli overlooking the town a hotshot, New York-based U.S. trader of Pacific Rim currencies who was openly boasting about the large amount of cash – derived, he said, from illicit activities – that he had carried with him on his outbound flight and deposited in a Swiss bank.

It is, of course, Switzerland's reputation as a safe haven for funds whose origins, even now, are not too closely inquired into, that underlies the artificially high value of the Swiss franc. The occasional scandals involving Italian flight capital, laundered Mafia money, U.S. tax fraud or insider trading have not seriously eroded banking secrecy laws, although they have occasionally liberalized their interpretation – especially when the U.S. Justice Department or Securities and Exchange Commission has brought pressure to bear. I believe that it is a safe assumption that the banks unlucky enough to be caught represent but a small proportion of those accepting or even soliciting questionable deposits.

Other factors generally cited as contributing to a strong franc are political stability, competitive interest rates with low inflation and a rate of unemployment which is invariably the lowest in Europe. After the continental recession brought on by German reunification, the overall Swiss rate of *Arbeitslosigkeit* or unemployment reached only five and two-tenths percent, which was the highest since the end of the Second World War. Of course, the French and Italian cantons experienced unemployment rates of up to nine percent; thus the level in the German-speaking cantons was considerably lower than the national average.

But let us resume our narrative. When Credit Suisse's U.S. research function was finally transferred to a New York brokerage affiliate called Swiss American Securities Inc., or SASI – which continued to follow only a small fraction of the stocks we covered – Dr. Dellsperger, the aforementioned head of the department, told me that he thought that the bank, through the collaboration of its various affiliates associated with the U.S. financial markets, could 'solve' the difference between buy-side and sell-side research. It was clear from this remark that he did not understand the real differences involved.

For neophytes, the 'buy-side' consists of the banks and insurance companies which manage private and institutional accounts as well as pension funds and mutual funds; the sell-side is the array of brokerage houses which execute the buy-side's trades for commissions or 'soft' dollars, and which also engage in conflicting activities such as investment banking and corporate finance, which they attempt (with great success, usually) to facilitate by urging their buy-side clients to invest in the newly underwritten securities. In order to generate commissions, their analysts try to frighten institutional investors out of their best holdings by frequently changing their recommended holdings and model portfolios.

Institutional brokerage salesmen typically regard buy-side analysts as peons to be courted with expense-account lunches in the cause of helping them unload such new issues. Whether the analyst is cooperative or recalcitrant, the salesman also goes over his head and courts his bosses as well. For example, when I worked at Crocker Investment Management Corporation in San Francisco, the president and his wife were guests of a broker at the Sarajevo Winter Olympics; propriety and the Securities and Exchange Commission dictated that they provide their own airfare, which they did by cashing in some of their frequent flyer miles.

Such salesmen often provide additional services to an analyst's superiors on a confidential basis. For that reason, I never tell them anything that I would not want my employers to know. Catching on to this, some of them ask me pointed questions in front of my *Vorgesetzener* (literally, the person placed over me), e.g. 'How much do you pay in rent each month?' (In this case, I felt forced to provide the information.)

Goldman Sachs' employees are in the habit of taking notes on every buy-side analyst with whom they come into contact. Eventually, I believe, the firm builds a book on each analyst client, which it apparently shares with current or prospective employers. Was the analyst receptive to his counterparts' recommendations? Was he available for breakfast and dinner meetings regardless of his commuting arrangements, vacation schedule, or cultural commitments?

Private Swiss banks are not necessarily more client-friendly than the large, publicly owned ones. I have a friend, Henry Vallotton, an older Swiss, who once had a non-mandate account at a prominent private bank here. When one of his Swiss bonds began to appreciate as interest rates declined, the bank sold his bond, alleging that its price had peaked. Research proved this not to be the case. Henry complained, to no avail; only when he threatened legal action, and mentioned that he had retained an attorney, did the bank's chairman offer to settle for half the claim. Henry accepted; I wouldn't have. There was no mandate, no full discretion; it was strictly an investment account, with transactions to be directed solely by the client.

Of course, there are more ethical banks with good performance records. I worked for one, a private bank heavily owned by a large British commercial bank, and now overseen by an affable chief investment officer who is a nephew of Admiral Dönitz's second-in-command. (His family emigrated to Switzerland just as Hitler was coming to power; he was a child at the time.)

Although the analysts at this bank were first-rate, they occupied a lowly status, being assigned tiny offices and paid salaries half of the portfolio managers' level. They were under constraints never to change an opinion lest they lose 'credibility', and they seemed to exist in order to take the blame when an investment went sour, with portfolio managers getting the credit for acting upon successful recommendations. At weekly meetings of thirty or so investment staff in a small, unair-conditioned conference room in which, when the windows were closed in summer, I once nearly fainted from excessive carbon dioxide, the analysts would stand in the back of the room for the hour's duration of the meeting. After the foreign exchange trader had pontificated interminably and often incorrectly about the likely relative directions of mark, franc, yen and dollar, each analyst would be given about two minutes to make his contribution. It was clear to everyone in the room that the analysts were second-class colleagues.

This was brought home to me forcefully when I scheduled a presentation by a prominent visiting Street analyst and no one showed up at the appointed hour, not even those who had indicated interest. Half an hour into our private discussion, one senior portfolio manager straggled in, indignant that I had not telephoned him to issue a special invitation once the analyst had actually arrived lest he waste a precious moment by walking over too soon. Presumably, his cohorts were also balancing chips of wood on their shoulders. To make matters worse, when this manager immediately acted upon one of the visitor's recommendations, he directed the order to another brokerage house.

The secret of this bank's success, in any case, was not security selection, sector rotation or industry diversification, but rather asset allocation. With considerable help from international brokerage firms, the strategist correctly anticipated moves in real interest rates in major European markets and the policy committee adjusted the geographic distribution of assets in mandated accounts to profit from this analysis. Was the French rate of inflation below its long-term interest rates? Then the French franc would strengthen, and investments denominated in this currency need not be hedged (through derivatives). (The strategist stopped short of advising outright currency speculation à la George Soros.) Yes, management charges and transaction fees were high, but during epochs of sharply declining interest rates clients profited handsomely.

So did the bank's senior officers. In the annual report, available on conference room and waiting room tables to all visitors, it was disclosed that total compensation to employees had risen fifty percent during the preceding year. Since most employees received a four percent increase in salary and a ten percent increase in bonus, the large increases were clearly enjoyed by the top officers. Herman K., a career employee who had worked for a considerable time in the bookkeeping department, actually estimated each employee's salary and confirmed the conclusion I have described.

A word about asset allocation. Most Swiss banks diversify both financially and geographically, i.e. among cash, bonds and stocks as well as among national markets. A corollary of this is that the percentage of assets devoted to the U.S. market is generally between ten percent and twenty percent. If the entire U.S. allocation is in stocks then, in theory, given the fact that each investment must represent a sufficient proportion of the portfolio to affect its performance – three percent to four percent is usual – the typical balanced portfolio should hold between three and seven U.S. equities.

Moreover, even this small number may be reduced in practice. Swiss bankers resent the reporting requirements attached to U.S. investments, and their accountants dislike the partial withholding of dividends required for foreigners investing in U.S. equities. At the private bank for which I worked I was unable to convince the portfolio managers to invest in General Dynamics because the partial returns of capital represented by liquidating dividends were subject to withholding, and the process for recovering such amounts was so onerous that the managers would incur the wrath of their accountants if they followed my advice.

Similarly, most Swiss private banks (including the one I worked for) limit their U.S. accounts to no more than five so that they can escape the complicated reporting requirements that kick in above this level.

It follows then that – even if the U.S. component of each diversified portfolio is unique – it is somewhat of a luxury for a private bank to employ even one U.S. analyst. Indeed, the U.S. investment research function is increasingly being exported to stateside affiliates and brokers by nearly all Swiss banks, including the *Grossbanken* which welcome U.S. accounts.

Accordingly, although Union Bank of Switzerland and Swiss Bank Corporation still employ U.S. analysts, they have increased their American investment presence. In addition to its own U.S. offices, UBS owns Chase Investors in New York, and SBC recently purchased Brinson Partners in Chicago and elected Gary Brinson to its board of directors. Thus it is conceivable that the Swiss portfolio managers at these banks, as is already the case at Credit Suisse, will eventually lose their German-speaking resident analysts, and be forced to wait six hours until their New York offices open for business to request information which, expressed in English, many of them may not fully understand.

In contrast, the Swiss love to invest in Canada, no doubt by reason of a shared inferiority complex, but their ability to do so directly is limited. For example, one of the hottest groups of funds in Canada is managed by the Orbitex organization. An American or Canadian can directly purchase shares in their no-load, open-end funds, but a European investor must purchase them through the Altamira firm in Switzerland which has exclusive distribution rights, and which charges front-end fees ranging from two percent for institutions investing at least two million Swiss francs to nine percent for, say, an individual investor in Germany who is prepared to commit one-tenth of that amount.

The private bank I worked for induced clients to subscribe to a new natural resources fund invested solely in shares of Canadian companies. Higher-ups made two trips to Canada, and I went along on the second. The ground rules – highly unusual from an American perspective – were these: only First Dominion Securities could set the agenda and no company was too small to invest in, even if it operated out of rented offices and boasted no more than thirty million dollars in its bank account. That Fidelity had mined the territory several months ahead of us, that we were too late for the current cycle, or that truly liquid markets existed in the stocks of only three of the companies we visited – these considerations were deemed irrelevant by my two companions, who were compulsive smokers and heavy drinkers; not surprisingly, their favorite company was Anderson Exploration, whose chairman is widely regarded in Calgary as indulging in food and drink to dangerous excess. While my companions wined and dined clients, I, not being invited to accompany them, visited Banff and Lake Louise and caught a performance of *The Phantom of the Opera* in Vancouver. At the end of the week, while they took a helicopter ride around that city, I rented another car and drove to Whistler Mountain where I spent four glorious days hiking and swimming among the friendly western Canadians.

This points up an important contrast between Swiss and American businessmen. The Swiss do not understand the concept of junkets or boondoggles. There are no 'Kelly girls' à la Eaton, no Bungalow Sevens à la Milken. At the annual Consumer Analysts Conference in St. Petersburg, Florida in the late 1970s and early 1980s, the schedule for the final afternoon invariably included Kellogg or Carnation, neither of which ever made presentations to analysts, in order to give attendees an afternoon at the beach without alerting their bosses back home. The Swiss, in contrast, are all business, even at conferences in attractive mountain settings. Neither of my colleagues, who travel to Canada frequently, have ever seen Banff, Lake Louise or Whistler Mountain. (Those executives who do go for recreation prefer to heli-ski in remote areas of the Canadian Rockies.)

As I wrote this, at the beginning of the second week of March, 1996, the business community in Switzerland was agog at the news that Sandoz and Ciba-Geigy were planning to ask shareholders to approve a merger of their pharmaceutical, agronomic and nutritional businesses. Five weeks later, the shareholders approved enthusiastically. Upon the inevitable consummation of this merger, a full tithe of the combined worldwide workforces of the two firms will be made redundant, including three thousand employees in Basel, where both firms are headquartered. Many will fail to find new positions; even that employer of last resort, the railroad, is already full of ex-bank employees. (The trains' punctuality, which had slipped a bit, has returned to normal.)

One month later, the Union Bank of Switzerland rejected an urgent merger proposal from CS Holding, which owns Credit Suisse, and was then itself rebuffed by the Swiss Bank Corporation, thus lending plausibility to my long-held expectation that someday Credit Suisse would propose a merger to the Swiss Bank Corporation in a desperate bid to regain the two banks' lost triple-A ratings on a combined basis. In 1997, Union Bank of Switzerland and Swiss Bank Corporation agreed to merge, subject to various regulatory approvals, which at this writing are pending. In 1998, the U.S. firms Citicorp and Travelers followed this example, thus continuing the contest to create the world's largest financial institution.

Credit Suisse, with the lowest ratio of equity to assets of the three major banks, has apparently overextended itself somewhat through the aggressive acquisitions of its CS Holding Corporation: in Switzerland alone, CS Holding already owns Swiss Volksbank, Bank Leu, Clariden Bank, Bank Hofmann, Neumünster Bank, Aargauer Bank and Handelsbank und Industrie, and it is now 'integrating' the operations of Volksbank and Bank Leu with those of Credit Suisse, eliminating two of every three jobs at the two smaller banks and in the process throwing hundreds out of work. In asset management, Dr. Peter Dellsperger has been promoted to chief investment officer and placed in charge of this downsizing. Even at the parent bank, the future of such areas as private banking and North American commercial banking lies in doubt, and the research department has eliminated secondary research on all non-Swiss markets and focused only on primary research on Swiss stocks; a few analysts following other markets were absorbed by private banking units. But the Elliott Wave team, now expanded to three persons, survives, and continues to spend good bank money advertising its plagiarized and – in my opinion – wholly useless product.

In the same month – April, 1996 – Swissair proposed eliminating all of its transcontinental flights serving Geneva. In early May, the Swiss post office, the PTT, announced plans to close branches and to lay off ten thousand employees. In mid-May, two major breweries, Hürlimann and Feldschlösschen, announced plans to merge. In September, the canton of Zürich announced a year-end pay reduction for all civic employees of three percent and ordered health and casualty insurers to refund up to eleven and a half percent of their 1996 premiums by the end of the year. In October, the engineering firm Sulzer dismissed nine hundred and fifty workers. At the end of November, Swissair threatened to file for bankruptcy unless the regime provided assistance. In December, the Union Bank of Switzerland announced that it would take an extraordinary provision for bad loans, report a loss for the year and eliminate eight hundred jobs over the next two years. As a result, the bank was immediately placed on Standard & Poors' Credit Watch with negative implications.

Clearly, the downward trend of the Swiss economy is snowballing, but this is not yet reflected in the official unemployment rate, currently 4.7%, because of the unusually large number of chronic unemployed (beyond two years) who have dropped off the rolls. The basic consumer interest rate on unrestricted funds is one percent or less, and fixed mortgage rates are scheduled to fall one-half percent, to 4.5%, in mid-summer. From my perspective, a bet on substantial devaluation of the Swiss franc over the medium to longer term seems desirable, even after the franc's thirteen percent decline relative to the U.S. dollar in the three months following 10th December, the day on which Cable News Network first aired a program entitled 'The Struggling Swiss Economy'. By 15th February, the Swiss franc had dropped thirty-six percent from its September level.

Swiss hotels, restaurants and cafés are already feeling the pinch of the rising unemployment, both actual and prospective, which has inevitably caused a decline in consumer confidence and spending. The summer of 1996 marked a nadir in tourist spending in the country, and September in particular recorded the lowest hotel volume in thirty-one years. In my neighborhood, whose shops are patronized by the wealthiest Swiss in Zürich, a wine shop, a top of the range stereo store and a famous gourmet butcher shop (whose decline was sharply accelerated by the scare surrounding 'mad cow' disease which has afflicted nearly as many Swiss cattle as British) are already numbered among the casualties, which are just starting to mount. Thriving instead are used clothing stores (Carol's Second Hand Shop at Stadelhofen is my favorite, but where is her first hand shop?), flea markets – the one on Saturdays at Bürkliplatz in Zürich keeps expanding, and in addition to clothing and glassware now offers lighting fixtures, paintings and compact discs for two francs – and noontime movies, which are an innovation here.

After a ten-year lag, the Swiss economic landscape is thus beginning to resemble the U.S. economy of the 1980s. Thousands of jobs are being sacrificed in order, say, that Hoffmann La Roche's quarterly earnings gains reach eighteen percent instead of sixteen percent. In fact, we Americans taught the Swiss this restructuring craze, which is not capitalism at its finest, and Michael Milken does not deserve all of the blame. In the long run, Michael Douglas' movie portrayal of Gordon Gekko notwithstanding, greed is *not* good. Where there used to be six major banks in California, there are now two, Bank of America and Wells Fargo. Like their thousands of laid-off employees, hundreds of whom[2] still apply for each position that becomes available, the casualties had names which are swiftly being forgotten: Crocker Bank, Barclays Bank of California, Security Pacific and First Interstate Bank (which I always thought of as First Intestate Bank, the bank without balls).

I close this chapter with a tribute to the memory of my favorite Swiss institutional broker, a most pleasant, friendly and open chap named George Baumann, who committed suicide in September, 1996 for reasons unknown. Persistent rumors, invariably denied by his family, swirl around various types of cancer, including that of the lungs; he had not smoked for more than twenty years. My own view is that he could no longer pretend that his aspirations – e.g. to own property in a Spanish resort town – had been realized. He was managing the C.J. Lawrence/Morgan Grenfell office of Deutsche Bank. He had previously headed up First Boston's Zürich office, which was closed in an economy move by an official in London, as well as the local office of Kidder, Peabody, which was assimilated into Paine Webber. Three days before his death he had met with his superior from New York, who complimented him on the good August volume, according to a female colleague, who

[2]Representative documentation for this assertion is provided by Ken Gregory of Litman/Gregory of Larkspur, California, whose kind response of 8th May, 1997, to my application for an advertised position reads, in part: 'The job generated great interest and we received several hundred responses. After interviewing many qualified candidates over the past few weeks, we have filled the position.' Simultaneously, more than a decade after selling Crocker Investment Management Corporation to Fred Alger, Wells Fargo staffed up its new Wells Capital Management Unit with a handful of local professionals, who reported equally intense competition

reports, however, that he had been depressed for about a month. He was fifty-six years old, left a wife, a mother and various aunts and uncles, but no children. Until his passing, he had been most successful at the game of musical chairs, finding new jobs well into his fifties.

I attended his moving graveside funeral in the Zürcher Oberland town of Maur, as did an impressive number of colleagues, competitors, and customers. The service included a recitation of the Lord's Prayer in German, plus two trumpet voluntaries, one chosen by the deceased some twenty years previously, and titled 'Green Grass', the other a version of taps complete with flourishes and riffs. Afterward, the Catholic priest officiated at a mass in the adjacent Reform church – a rare act of ecumenism in the canton of Zürich, in which none of the Reform cathedrals are available for Catholic weddings.

George harbored absolutely no prejudices; any rough edges which once existed had been polished in the crucible of a business career. He was the only Swiss broker who was willing to recommend me for a position at his own firm, as a biotechnology analyst. I expressed interest when the incumbent left shortly before the Zürich performance of a 'dog and pony show' for a biotech firm seeking to raise funds. At the event, I met a young, cheerful investment banker surnamed Lloyd-Harris, apparently of European origin, who had legally changed his given name to 'Genghis', and who informed me that my first duty if I were hired would be to recommend the shares of the visiting company. Talk about conflicts of interest! In the event, lacking portable clients, I was not hired for the position, but it was good to meet the reborn explorer.

Chapter V
The Pleasures of Berner Oberland and Central Switzerland

The world is too much with us; late and soon,
Getting and spending, we lay waste our powers:
Little we see in Nature that is ours;
We have given our hearts away, a sordid boon!

William Wordsworth

Berner Oberland, as the name implies, is the canton encompassing the mountains upriver from Bern, and it is the most popular vacation destination for many tourists, including Americans. It includes the popular town of Interlaken, which lies, as its name suggests, between two lakes: *Brienzersee*, or the Lake of Brienz, and *Thunersee*, or the Lake of Thun. Through both lakes, in this order, flows the River Aare, which warms up as it leaves the mountains so that it is much more comfortable to swim in the Lake of Thun than in the Lake of Brienz. From the mountains above the lakes you can see a striking contrast: the Lake of Thun, being warmer, is blue, while the Lake of Brienz, being colder and also deeper, is green.

At the other end of the Interlaken valley, past the far end of the Brienzersee, and technically in central Switzerland, is the charming and less well-known resort town of Meiringen, which is a good place to establish headquarters in the area; I recommend staying at the dryly named Sherpa Hotel, next to which is one of the town's several mountaineering shops, this one called the Glatthard. Between Meiringen and Innertkirchen you can walk along part of the gorge cut by the Aare and there is a campground at the end near Innertkirchen. From a number of bus stops in this area, a *Postauto* (postbus) will take you to the mountain valley called Engstlenalp (near the small lake Engstlensee) above Innertkirchen, and from there you can walk over the Jochpass to Engelberg, site of the Titlis ski area, allegedly (and apocryphally) named in honor of Swiss-German women.

Or, instead – and this is one of my favorite hikes – you can walk past the hotel and via the lakes Tannensee and Melchsee to the small but charming Frutt ski area in central Switzerland. As you approach Frutt from Engstlenalp on the right-hand side you will see the Stocklialp cable car, which can carry you to a restaurant high on the saddle overlooking Frutt, as well as a gondola which climbs over the saddle and descends on the opposite side to the Melchtal. Past the hotels at Frutt there is also a small ski lift, the Bonistock. On the left side of the valley there is a long, single chair lift which climbs to the scenic Balmeregghorn, to the right of which a saddle leads in less than an hour to Planplatten, which lies at the top of the larger and more popular Hasliberg ski area. From Planplatten you can take a double chair lift down to Mäggisalp, where a terrace restaurant overlooks the Meiringen valley in the afternoon sun. From Mäggisalp a gondola continues down through Bidmialp to Reuti, whence a cable car takes you back to Meiringen, within a five-minute walk of the center, the lower end of the Aare gorge or the parking lot on the side of town nearest to

Innertkirchen. (Alternatively, Reuti and its own small parking lot are accessible by road from the Brünig pass, just before the turnoff to Meiringen.)

A variation on the above is to turn left at the Tannensee on the path which leads directly to Planplatten, bypassing the Melchsee and Frutt.

A third walk from Engstlenalp leads past the near end of the Engstlensee up to a saddle called, appropriately, Sattli. A somewhat steep trail down the other side leads to a most pleasant mountain restaurant, the Tallihütte, facing the Süsten valley, the towns Fuhren and Gadmen and the afternoon sun. The challenge is staying on the trails below the restaurant down to the valley, which is farther than it looks. I don't recommend it: instead, beg a ride from someone who has driven to the restaurant along the small private road, or walk down the road itself. There is also a primitive mountain hut nearby; avoid it.

Other postautos will take you to scenic trailheads along the Süsten and Grimsel passes above Meiringen. The Rosenlaui-Schwarzenberg bus route along the Süsten pass ends at a trailhead from which you can climb to Grosse Scheidegg and thence take another bus either to Grindelwald or back to Meiringen; alternatively, you can walk down to the First lift and ride it to Grindelwald. The bus which traverses the Grimsel pass will let you off at the bottom of the Siedelhorn, from the top of which on clear days you can see the Matterhorn high above Zermatt; Cervinia, Italy is on the other side. You can either retrace your steps or walk down the other side of the Siedelhorn to the Wallis (or Valais) side of the Grimsel pass and then take a bus back over the pass to Meiringen.

Yet another spectacular hike begins at the peak of the Stockhorn mountain, reached by aerial tramway from Erlenbach, accessible by car or a train from Thun and located in the lovely Simmen valley which leads to

Zweisimmen and the Rinderberg ski area, Schön Ried (home of an American school) and the interconnected Horneggli ski piste, and the famed resort of Gstaad. The panoramic trail from the Stockhorn winds above meadows melodious with cow bells to the Leiteren pass, on the other side of which is a postauto stop and, a bit further, the popular Gurnigel restaurant and hostel. Either from a hobbyist flying a remote controlled toy airplane above Gurnigel or from a diner at the restaurant you can easily obtain a ride to Thun, thus eliminating the need to ride the postauto to Bern, which in any case must be reserved in advance.

In Interlaken itself the Casino Hotel is the site of summer concerts, and in the large park across the street from the main entrance there are organized fireworks on the night of 1st August, Swiss National Day, beginning around 9:30 p.m. (By contrast, the fireworks in Zürich in the park along the lake are highly individual events, with Roman candles purchased at the supermarket chains Migros or the Coop [only the latter sells alcoholic beverages] likely to be thrown across your path as you stroll along; amazingly, I have never heard of injuries at this annual event.) If you watch the display in Interlaken – and I recommend that you do – and then drive back to Zürich over the Brünig pass toward Lucerne, you will be treated to additional incandescences along the way. Just above Giswil, on the left-hand side as you drive toward Lucerne, there is an elegant restaurant, the Landhaus, for leisurely dining.

High above Giswil, also in central Switzerland, is a panoramic mountain road which leads past Mörlialp and Sörenberg over the Glaubenbüelen pass, at the top of which is a parking lot and a network of hiking trails, one of which leads in fifteen minutes to a garden restaurant. The other side of the pass leads to the Brienzer Rothorn ski area, accessible for summer hiking via a cable car which leads to a restaurant at the top. Two cog railways wind down to the valley of Brienz below. The views of the lake of Brienz are breathtaking on a sunny afternoon. Beyond the ski area the road continues down to the Emmental valley (home of the famous cheese) between Lucerne and Bern.

If you turn left, in the direction of Bern, and continue for perhaps twenty kilometers to the village of Trubschachen, then turn right toward Trub and Fankhaus, the narrow road leads to Mettlenalp, where you can park, have lunch at the restaurant there and choose either of two trails (the shorter and steeper one takes fifty minutes, the longer, gentler dirt road an hour and a quarter) up to a low mountain (at fourteen hundred eight meters) called Napf, which has scenic views of the lakes near Giswil and the main crest of the Alps to the south, and which also has, yes, a restaurant. From Napf there is a network of trails to Entlebuch in the Emmental as well as to other passes and high forest villages.

In German, the word for the expression I just used, 'the main crest of the Alps', is *Alpenhauptkamm*. The word *Kamm*, like its etymological equivalent in English, means comb or crest, and can be used to refer to a rooster's crest as well as a comb for the hair. If you walk along the dirt road from Napf back to Mettlenalp on a day when the near Alpine crest to the south has a light dusting of snow, it does look exactly like the tines of a comb and it is extremely beautiful, especially in late afternoon.

High above Interlaken is Beatenberg, accessible thence by car or postbus, or, from Beatenbucht on the lake, by funicular, with mapped views from the top of the Niederhorn of virtually all the major Alpine peaks in Switzerland and even Mont Blanc in France: good hiking, with plenty of opportunity to see deer, chamois, steinboks (ibexes, a kind of antelope), and *Murmeltiern*, or marmots, which greet you with their distinctive whistle; plus excellent restaurants. From the top of the ski lift in Beatenberg one can walk to the Gemmenalphorn, which overlooks the Justiztal, or Justice Valley, and then walk down this valley back to Beatenberg or further down to Merligen on the lake of Thun. The British influence is apparent here in the presence of a few cairns near the Gemmenalphorn; aside from Zermatt, I have seen them nowhere else in Switzerland.

Two variations at somewhat lower elevations (around seventeen hundred meters above sea level) both start at Innereriz, accessible by bus from Thun, one leading over the Sichel saddle to the Justiztal and the other traversing the Zettenalp pass to Schwanden and Sigriswil above Gunten, farther down the lake toward Thun. This last hike is popular with accompanied groups of school children, who have lunch in Sigriswil and then take postbuses to Gunten and Thun. I would avoid the misnamed Grünenberg pass, situated in the forest between the Gemmenalphorn and Innereriz, as the path down to Innereriz is hard to follow, involves climbing over or crawling under at least one barbed wire fence and traversing a richly manured farm pen occupied by one hyper-friendly pig, a cow and a horse.

High above the other side of the lakes are the popular year-round resorts of Grindelwald, Lauterbrunnen and Mürren. The last is the setting for James Bond's picturesque escape on skis from his pursuers in the movie *On Her Majesty's Secret Service*, and offers one of the longest ski runs in Europe. Beyond Lauterbrunnen are the Trümmelbach waterfalls, with impressive views along a staircase of the falls' power and, at the end of the road, the town of Stechelberg. Further beyond it are hiking trails and a hotel accessible only by foot or horse. Both Lauterbrunnen and Stechelberg have campgrounds, with the former offering a cafeteria and beautiful views of nearby waterfalls. Both towns offer transportation up to Mürren, six hundred meters above the valley, and to which you cannot drive.

Mürren has splendid views of the Eiger, Mönch, and Jungfrau peaks, across the valley, and these views are incorporated in some lovely hotels, including the luxurious Eiger and the more affordable Edelweiss, which always has a five-star chef, and which is owned by a charming young woman named Sandra von Allmend. I recommend both. When you stay at any hotel in Mürren, you may use the town's sport facility for free, which includes a gymnasium, large indoor swimming pool with unisex locker room and showers, and outdoor skating and curling rinks. In winter, there are figure ice skating competitions for children, complete with costumes, judges and musical programs. These begin in late morning, at around eleven o'clock, and are so charming that they are worth giving up half a day's skiing to watch.

Mürren is an English town, with memorabilia of Sherlock Holmes. The English are competitive; they rope off parts of the best pistes and charge a few francs to time your speed as you race through the slalom poles they erect, and they sponsor a famous race known as the Palace Run from the Piz Gloria summit of the Schilthorn mountain (site of a panoramic restaurant) down to the town. Some of the most difficult ski runs bear English names. There is even a resident 'leader' of the grandly named Ski Club of Great Britain – sometimes, reflecting upon the loss of empire, I am tempted to ask, 'What's great about it?' – who posts a daily schedule in hopes of attracting 'followers'.

Don't join such groups, as you will invariably be limited to the pace of the least talented skier, who probably will have forgotten her poles and have to go back and get them while you wait. The leader, normally a woman escaping her husband and children for the winter, will lecture you about the dangers of skiing alone. Ignore her: not being Swiss, she knows nothing about it. The Swiss take their children on off-piste powder tours without a guide. Whenever I encounter such follow-the-leader's-S-turns groups, I ski past them singing 'All We Like Sheep' at the top of my voice, just as I used to do when riding a bicycle in San Francisco's Golden Gate Park against a tide of one hundred thousand joggers wearing T-shirts proclaiming 'Gay Liberation'.

If you like to ski on powder snow, I recommend that you stay at either the Edelweiss in Mürren or the Silberhorn in Lauterbrunnen, perched on the hill above the train station and also owned by a family named von Allmend, which means 'from the Alps'. By advance reservation, either Sandra's father at the Edelweiss, usually on Wednesdays, or the Grindelwald ski school on weekends (if you start in Grindelwald, Wengen, Kleine Scheidegg, Lauterbrunnen, Wilderswil, or Interlaken Ost) offer guided tours which begin at the Jungfraujoch (at 3,450 meters above sea level) just over the Wallis or Valais side of the border with Berner Oberland. The train that takes you there features a couple of scenic stops along the way, announced in comments recorded in seven languages, including Italian, Spanish, Japanese and Chinese.

In the first such tour, you ski down a broad expanse, which looks like a natural highway, to 2,900 meters at Concordia Platz (locus of John McPhee's book on the Swiss army, *La Place de la Concorde Suisse*, which is French for Concordia Platz). From there you climb (with synthetic skins which prevent backsliding and extra snap-in bindings which leave your heels free for climbing, and which you carry, along with lunch, in a *Rücksack* or backpack) for a couple of hours to the 3,200 meter high Lötschenlücke gap, whence you ski down the Lang glacier to Blatten, a charming village at the end of the Lötschental valley. There you should have a few Gurten beers (I prefer the dark gold version when available) at the Silberdistel (Silver Thistle) restaurant before taking the postbus back to Goppenstein and the train back through Spiez to Interlaken, Lauterbrunnen or another starting point.

It is also possible to take this tour without a guide but, because the winds and snows usually obliterate the previous day's trail from the Jungfraujoch, I recommend joining the ski school group at least as far as Concordia Platz, whence a trail up to the top of the gap is generally visible.

The second guided tour, which has a bit of climbing at the end but does not involve the need for skins and extra bindings, begins in the same way but then takes you on past Concordia Platz down the Aletsch glacier, past the sunken armory described in McPhee's book, to Rieder Furka above the beautiful Rhône (or Valais) valley, whence you take a ski lift to Mörel and a train through Brig back to your starting point. I warn you, though, that this second route has many more crevasses, and should not be attempted without a guide.

In summer hikes along this latter route, one generally leaves the glacier on the afternoon of the second day by climbing to the Mariellensee, a lake, along a path which leads to Kuhboden above the Valais, with the option of continuing on to Rieder Furka on either the glacier or the Valais side on one's own. You can stay at the Alpina Hotel in Kuhboden or choose from the hotels in the Valais town of Fiesch below, accessible by cable car.

I spoke of a 'second day' above for good reason. This hike involves a mandatory overnight stay at the very primitive Concordia Hut, above the opposite side of the valley from the Lötschenlücke. If you go there on the afternoon before a full moon rises above the Lötschenlücke, as I did, the evening and nocturnal views from the porch are memorable. As it can be cold on a glacier even in summer, be sure to bring a ski parka, cap and gloves; your own sheets, pillow case and bottled water (for brushing your teeth as well as drinking); plus a sandwich, candy bar and beverages for the next day.

This hike *must* be arranged through the ski school. For protection from crevasses through which one can fall forty meters to a river below – avoid innocent-looking patches of earth covered with a dollop of snow – each hiker is looped around the waist with a rope attached similarly to several other hikers of both sexes, with a guide in front. The walks last for about three and a half hours on the first day, when you begin in mid-afternoon, and for six hours on the second, when you begin walking shortly after six o'clock in the morning because at lower altitudes the glacier becomes too soft for safety later in the day. If your bladder is at all like mine, this second day can prove quite challenging – especially in view of the need to drink large quantities of liquid in order to avoid dehydration in the Alps, above the atmosphere.

Because of this thinness of atmosphere, you must also use adequate sunscreen protection, no matter how swarthy your skin is. I advise a couple of coats of a cream lotion in the morning, followed by two or three applications of a greasy ointment such as Piz Buin or Roc, with SPF of fifteen or twenty. All exposed skin should be so treated, including not only face, neck and ears but also hands, since you will be taking off your gloves to eat lunch, change bindings, etc.

A beautiful five-hour hike for which you need no guide is from Schynige Platte, which is reached by train from Wilderswil (between Interlaken Ost and Lauterbrunnen), to the Faulhorn high above Grindelwald, and thence down to the First chair lift, the longest in Switzerland, which takes you down to Grindelwald. I recommend taking the early morning train, which leaves Wilderswil at a quarter to eight, and having breakfast at the hotel in Schynige Platte.

Alternatively, you could take the late afternoon train there and stay overnight, especially if the moon is full. Unlike many Alpine hikes that circle around a single valley, this traverses several, with short detours which have spectacular views of the green and blue lakes (of Brienz and Thun) far below. There is a small restaurant (the Weberhütte, owned until 1997 by Frau Weber) at the junction from which you begin the climb to the Faulhorn, which also has a hotel-restaurant but not one I would recommend, especially for overnight stays, as it is rather primitive, although the views of the full moon are just as awesome as from Schynige Platte.

Twice a year, weather permitting, on the Saturday nights closest to the full moons of July and August, there are accompanied all-night hikes along this route. The train leaves Wilderswil at eleven o'clock at night, and when you arrive at Schynige Platte forty-five minutes later you will find the hotel and restaurant open. Everyone eats a second dinner, and most people begin walking in small groups around one o'clock. If the night stays clear, you will not need a flashlight: by the light of the moon you can clearly see not only the trail but even the lakes (though not their colors) below! You should reach the Faulhorn about fifty minutes before sunrise; the moonfall can be even more spectacular. After sunrise, around six o'clock, you walk for another two hours past chamois and sheep down to the First chair lift, which opens at eight.

I would spend the next day relaxing on the shore of the Lake of Thun at either the public (free) or private (a modest fee is charged) grassy 'beach' belonging to the Hotel Neuhaus, which can be reached by car or lake steamer. There are campgrounds and restaurants within walking distance and the Neuhaus itself is lovely, with a lakeside restaurant. I also suggest that you try the Landhaus restaurant, which is a short walk along the lake through a campground. (The Landhaus serves Eichhof Hubertus dark beer, comparable with Gurten dark gold.) There are river walks as well, to Interlaken and beyond. And the Lake of Thun is one of the three or four cleanest in Switzerland, together with the lakes of Zürich (the *Zürichsee*) and Lucerne (the *Vierwallstättersee*), and the small but lovely and islanded *Kaumasee* below Flims in Graubünden.

On the way to Berner Oberland from Bern, I recommend that you turn off at the exit marked 'Rubingen, Muri, Belp' and follow the sign toward Belp, home of Gurten beer. Just after you cross the Aare, take the second right turn (marked with a small sign) to the Restaurant Campagna, which has an outdoor terrace right on the river. The house specialty is *Forelle Baretti*, or trout amandine, and the trout are taken live and fresh from the fishery across the river. There is also an outdoor barbecue. For dessert, try the pineapple shell stuffed with ice cream and chunks of the fruit. The parasols will remind you to order Gurten beer.

Chapter VI
Zermatt, the Glory of Wallis

Über allen Gipfeln
Ist Ruh.
In allen Wipfeln
Spürest du
Kaum einen Hauch;
Die Vögelein schweigen im Walde.
Warte nur, balde
Ruhest du auch.

Peace descends upon the hills.
There rises from rooftops a bare wisp of smoke.
The woodland birds are in slumber.
Be patient: soon rest will enfold you in peace.

Goethe

It is difficult to reach Zermatt, but well worth it. From Zürich you motor past Bern to Kandersteg, where you drive onto a flatcar train and sit in darkness for a quarter of an hour, while the train takes you through the Lötschberg tunnel. Thence you drive toward Visp and take the turn off to Zermatt, but you must leave your car in a parking lot at Täsch and take another train for another quarter of an hour to Zermatt. At both Täsch and Zermatt there are carts (or kulis, as they are called) available for a refundable deposit of five francs. If you arrive in Täsch on a Saturday morning during ski season, you are likely to find the main lot full but you must nonetheless stop there, pay for the anticipated length of your stay, then drive a mile back to a secondary lot, park and take a bus back. This can take an hour. Most people leave their luggage at the main lot while moving the car; amazingly, nothing is ever stolen.

From Lucerne, you motor to Andermatt, again drive onto a flatcar train which traverses the Furka tunnel to the end of the lovely Rhône valley described in the previous chapter, down to Brig, around to Visp and up to Täsch. The Glacier Express, which begins in St. Moritz and goes through Davos, Klosters and Chur, follows this route all the way to Zermatt. Its first-class cars have dome roofs and the entire train has a recorded description of notable sights along the way in English, German, and French.

In Zermatt itself there are virtually no automobiles. Residents are permitted to drive through Täsch to a garage at the end of the town, and some tourists ignore the warning sign and do so as well but they risk a heavy fine. Instead of cars there are electric carts and, for the wealthy, horse-drawn buggies. There are excellent restaurants, hotels and pubs with American music. Avoid the hotels near the train station and go up the main street toward the church. On your way, you will pass Grampi's Pub on the right-hand side as well as the Gitan gourmet restaurant at the Darioli Hotel, and on the left-hand side some interesting boutiques, the Broken Ski Bar in the Hotel de la Poste (which caters to young singles and offers nightly entertainment), plus two world-class hotels, Seiler's Mont Cervin (which is French for Matterhorn) and the Zermatterhof. At the latter, swimming in the pool must allegedly be done in the nude.

Just before the church, turn left and cross the bridge. There you will find two of the best, reasonably priced hotels, the Bristol and, past the Papperla Pub to the left, the

Aristella, with its excellent Spycher Restaurant, which serves Cardinal beer. (Unlike many such hotels that cater primarily to middle-class Germans, who generally eschew lamb but relish *Schwein*, both of these serve lamb.) At the Papperla, American rock-and-roll is always to be found, and the bartenders make a fantastic, chuggable drink called a 'hot shot', composed of Irish coffee made with Galliano liquor and heavy cream and served in a shot glass.

The few exceptions to this concentration of the best establishments are the da Mario restaurant in the elegant Schweizerhof Hotel near the station; the Hotel Alpenhof, along the river and across from the Sunegga ski lift; next to it, the Cheminée restaurant in the hotel of that name, which features U.S. beefsteaks and *carreé d'agneau*, rack of lamb; the nearby Le Mazot restaurant, which also specializes in lamb; and the shops on the cross street to the left (including the Jo-Na ski glove shop) which leads past the Vernissage movie theater and bar to the skating and curling rinks.

There are classical concerts at the Zermatterhof Hotel, for which evening attire is standard. At the other extreme, there are three restaurants on the descent from Sunegga where you can dine in your ski clothes: Othmar's Hütte for lunch; da Leonardo for lunch and, on certain Tuesday nights, Italian dinners; and the Canadian Bernie Jacob's Olympia Stübli for both meals every day, with a true rarity as the house specialty – *Poulet in Chorbli*, or fried chicken in the basket. The Olympia Stübli often has American rock-and-roll singers in mid-to-late afternoon, when the views of the town and, in the distance, the Matterhorn are especially spectacular.

The ski school offers off-piste tours on three glaciers. The first involves a ninety-minute climb above the top of the Stockhorn and circles around to the Platten and Triftje lifts. The second goes over the peak above Klein

Matterhorn and comes down above Trockener Steg. And the third takes you by helicopter to the top of the Monte Rosa, whence you ski down to Trockener Steg. There are variations on these themes as well.

Zermatt has four distinct ski areas within the bounds of the pistes. The best, and most challenging, is the area around the Rothorn and Stockhorn peaks, including the popular Triftje-Platten-Gant area, with a young, colorfully designer-dressed, upper-class clientele who *wedeln* down the formidable Triftje bumps. (The Triftje lift was closed for six weeks in early 1997 after a serious accident in which the cable came off the rollers and injured a skier's shoulder; local hotel owners attribute this apocryphally to a failed attempt by two skiers to board the lift at a plateau above its starting point: when they released the T-bar, it allegedly swung all the way over the main cable and caught at the next tower. The moral of this propaganda is: Don't swing while riding any ski lift.) Above Gant is a sunny and deservedly popular terraced restaurant, the Grünsee, formerly known as the Findelgletscher, with decent food, reasonable prices, occasional entertainment and now and then a fantastic *ananas boule* dessert, consisting of chunks of pineapple in a glass of champagne, Malibu and kirsch. At the end of the day, take the Rothorn lift and ski down the Kumme trail, with (in spring) its corn-snow moguls and spectacular views of the Täsch valley.

The Gornergrat area, served by a train and T-bars, has mostly easy runs and is mainly notable for its access to the Riffelalp Hotel (owned, like the Mont Cervin, by Seiler) whose outdoor terrace-restaurant is top-drawer. (Do not confuse this with the Riffelberg cafeteria, higher up the train line, and do not be surprised, as you ride a crowded morning train up the mountain, to observe that the men and the young commonly sit while women and the old remain standing.) In the early morning, the run from

Gornergrat to Grünsee is virtually empty and memorably beautiful, with an incredibly lovely view of the Matterhorn. Gornergrat is also accessible from the Rote Nase cable car, which is a two-minute climb above the Triftje bumps: one travels to the Hohtälli terminus and, via additional cable cars, on to Gornergrat or the Stockhorn. (The two cable cars to the Stockhorn are ancient, with visibly rusting roofs, and they often require recharging with an electric cord before each round trip.) From Hohtälli there are advanced runs to Grünsee (off-piste, powder or granular) and to Gant (the Mittel Ritz piste, full of challenging moguls) and an easier run (ending with a rope tow along a nearly level plateau) back to Riffelalp.

If you choose the Hohtälli-Grünsee run you can continue down the steep Börter piste which begins at the left of the restaurant to the chair lift below Findeln (which has a few eating places of its own), ride up to Sunegga and ski down the Rio mogul run, past the Olympia Stübli restaurant and on to Zermatt. Alternatively, you can ski to Gant, ride the gondola up to Blauherd and ski to Sunegga, past the Othmar's Hütte, Da Leonardo and Olympia Stübli restaurants, and on to Zermatt. Under good conditions, it is also possible to cross the bridge at Gant and ski directly to Findeln, down to the bottom of the chair lift and on to Findelbach, the first station on the Gornergrat line, from which there is a crossover to the trail descending from Furi to Zermatt.

Schwarzeealp, on the right side of the valley as you face the Matterhorn, is popular with older Germans, offers a cafeteria and has mostly gentle slopes, with the exception of one expert *Pukelpiste* or mogul run, the Mamatt, which leads right from near the bottom of the Hörnli lift down to Furi. On both sides of this junction there are a number of excellent restaurants, all with outdoor terraces: the Alm, which serves fresh *Forelle* or trout daily; above it, the Ritti, appropriate for a tête-à-tête; below it, the Moos, most suitable for a beer in the sun on the way down to town; and, on the other side, the Blatten (which specializes in lamb) and Zum See restaurants. The latter serves a delicious *Topf*, or potato soup with a baked cheese topping in a pot. You will pass other fuel stops as well, but I don't recommend any of them.

Furi, in turn, is the first station on the way up to the Klein Matterhorn at thirty-eight hundred meters, from which one can choose among the following possibilities: ski back down to the Gandegghütte, a pleasant terraced restaurant above the Trockener Steg station, dine and continue on skis to Furgg, whence the Garten T-bar takes you to a choice of off-piste powder or memorable moguls back to Furgg. From there, the descent to Furi offers challenging curves, a few bumps and striking views of the Zermatt valley. Alternatively, at the last T-bar leading to the Theodul glacier at the border, purchase a special pass and ski in the opposite direction past the Italian side of the Matterhorn and down a lovely river valley to Cervinia, have lunch and (with the special pass) take the lifts back to the Swiss side. Be warned, however, that the return trip can easily take two and a half hours on a weekend afternoon, and that the skiers and restaurateurs you will encounter – mostly Milanese who consider themselves Lombards rather than Italians – are not the most elegant, friendly or even honest representatives of their country, and they are strikingly different from the affluent skiers of Torino who throng to Lagalp and Diavolezza in the Engadin.

Another caveat: Zermatt, which is a relatively expensive resort, tends to attract wealthy and highly aggressive Germans. Do not be surprised to be pushed off lifts or elevators by a shove from a large German stomach, or to be asked to vacate your regular choice table in the hotel's dining room because a self-important German businessman has requested it for his family. The *Boche* will regularly push ahead of you in lift lines and at ticket counters. I generally tell them, in English, to go back to Germany. They add an unpleasant degree of hassle to an otherwise lovely resort town.

Unfortunately, however, the Swiss economy is to a large extent a reflection of the German one and, though sometimes tempting, it would be imprudent to exclude the overfed neighbors to the north – who regard Switzerland as their *Sudreich*, or southern province – from a major international resort. So watch out for that plump character behind you in the yellow ski suit as you approach the *Schlepplift* or T-bar. If he joins you on the lift, he will repeatedly knock his skis against yours, threaten your balance and give you loud and insistent orders about your posture. He is undoubtedly an engineer from Lübeck who has his own company and he is used to giving orders and having them obeyed. His rebellious son is probably a neo-Nazi skinhead. (The Swiss tolerate but don't really like the Germans, and I am reliably informed that the recent train wreck at Eschede gave rise to a certain *Schadenfreude* or perverse pleasure among many Swiss.)

When you leave Zermatt, especially in summer, an attractive variation is to drive to Brig and take the Simplon pass (or, in winter, the tunnel) to Italy, then drive to the Italian side of Lago Maggiore, circle around the lake to Locarno and take the especially beautiful San Bernadino pass back to Chur.

You can, of course, stay in Locarno, but the lake is so filthy that the insects it attracts will infect you with their bites. I've become ill the last three times I swam at the Lido pool in Locarno; virtually no one ventures into the lake any longer.

A better choice is to drive from Ascona (just beyond Locarno) up the Valley Maggia to the village of Maggia, drive over the bridge across the river, and swim from the rocks there. Be warned, however, that each spring when the river is full there are drownings. On the way you will pass Ponte Brolla, where there are two decent restaurants, the Centovalli and (yes) Mamma Mia's and, farther along, the Piccolo Paradiso campground and pizzeria at Avegno. Further up the valley is the ancient Roman town of Fusio, with picturesque restaurants and old dwellings, and above Fusio there is a network of hiking trails. In high summer, the Maggia River can become stagnant and smelly, while the nearby Verzasca River is said to retain its freshness.

Chapter VII
The Grandeur of Graubünden

An einen schönen Platz der Welt
Hab' dieses Haus ich hingestellt.
Doch niemals soll's mir aus dem Sinn
Daß ich hier nur ein Pilger bin.

At one of nature's loveliest places,
This house of mine the hillside graces,
But ne'er permit me to forget
That I am here a pilgrim set.

Sign painted on a house in Buchen

The largest canton in Switzerland is Graubünden, or Grisons in French, with the derivative Grischuna a common German adjective, as in *Chesa Grischuna*, a hotel in Klosters Platz popular with English and American visitors. Graubünden includes the popular Klosters-Davos ski areas, including foremost the shared Parsenn range with its seven on-piste village destinations; Jakobshorn, Pischa and Rinerhorn in Davos; and Madrisa (with a kindergarten) in Klosters Dorf. Adjacent to the Madrisa parking lot there is an excellent pizzeria, the *Al Berto*, which also serves succulent lamb chops and has a generously stocked salad bar.

Klosters Platz is the centerpiece and I have been traveling there to ski since the early 1970s when Swissair offered a week's ski package for two hundred and fifty dollars, including airfare, ground transportation, hotel, breakfast and dinner, and lift tickets – making it more economical to travel from the East Coast of the U.S. to Switzerland than to Colorado or Utah. Here is a catalogue of the village's delights:

Its best sauna, with lovely female bodies on view, is at the otherwise overrated Hotel Alpina.

Its best swimming pools are at the Hotel Sport near Klosters Dorf and the rather remote Hotel Pardenn at the edge of Klosters Platz.

Arguably its best Swiss kitchen is at the Wynegg (pronounced V-Neck) Hotel, owned by Ruth Guler, who taught the young Prince Charles to ski and attended his wedding, presenting him and poor Princess Diana with a cantonal wine cask. Minced veal and fondues are the specialties *de la maison*. (The Hotel Rustico's restaurant, featuring thick grilled lamb chops, offers serious competition from a different cuisine, as do those of the Steinbock, Chesa Grischuna and Walserhof hotels.)

Its best (and only) café is Fellini, which, oddly, doubles as a pizzeria, and which serves an excellent *Schokolade mélange*, or hot chocolate with whipped cream.

Its best chocolate shop is Schneider, just next door to Fellini.

Its best beer, in both light and dark varieties, as well as an *Eisbeer* type of dark ale, is Calanda.

Its best hard cider, or *Apfelwein*, which is also known as *Sauermost*, is Redinger; its best sweet cider, also known as *Süssmost*, is Obi.

Its best hard coffees – available only at the restaurant atop the highest peak reached by lifts, the Weissfluhgipfel – are the *Öpfelmues*, made with Gravensteiner apple brandy, and the 'Take me higher', containing Asbach Uralt *Weinbrand* or brandy, and served in especially designed, purchasable cups. By prearrangement, a first-rate paella can be ordered at this restaurant from Hedi Schwegler at least three days in advance for groups of four or more. The *Gipfel* is also the site of the worst-kept secret in Switzerland, a highly visible radar defense installation.

Partially because of the custom of Prince Charles, his sons William and Harry and entourage, Klosters is a wealthy ski resort. Virtually everyone wears a complete, matching ski suit. Brands of clothes and skis are more important even than in Zermatt, which is a more expensive resort. One will seldom feel conspicuous being well dressed in Klosters, whereas in smaller, less affluent areas a Killy or Bogner ski suit can bring unwelcome attention. Indeed, in the evenings one will see a number of mink coats, though fewer than in Zermatt, which attracts more non-skiers.

Klosters has several excellent ski shops: Köbi Böner's Gotschnasport, which I highly recommend; Casparis; and the more expensive Wunderlin's, formerly Hartmann's, whose aggressive proprietress was sometimes characterized by her English clientele as a combination of Lady Macbeth and Madame Defarge. However that may be, Hartmann's offered the best outer wool socks, Rohner silk undersocks, Sawaco silk-and-wool thermal underwear, and silk glove liners. Pierre Wunderlin and his partner Verena have modified the wares somewhat to reflect changing consumer tastes and preferences.

The upscale British and American tourists favor Conti *Mützen*, or caps, Reusch gloves, Kandahar or Blondo after-ski *Stiefel*, or boots, Medico cotton turtleneck shirts with zippers at the collar, and Killy ski suits. With regard to the latter, one should avoid the popular one-piece versions, which are heavy and too hot, since the jacket can never be removed or completely unzipped without exposing the wearer below the waist; for the same reason, one should also spurn the heavier, coarser models, which, being made of polyester rather than the relatively rare nylon (here called polyamide), 'breathe' so little that one emerges soaking wet on even the coldest, driest days.

For equipment, the cognoscenti incline toward K2 giant slalom skis and poles, Salomon ski boots and bindings, and French or Italian designer sunglasses. Fat Völkl touring skis and curved carving-skis are the current fads, but they are unnecessary for any but the deepest powder and perform terribly on prepared pistes.

In Graubünden, the 'beautiful' people, whether or not they ski, tend to go to Davos, where many Germans put on formal dress in the evenings and sit around the lobbies of the best hotels hoping to find a prince to take their ugly daughters off their hands. I was once invited to a concert in Davos for such a purpose and when I explained to the poor girl's father, whom I met eating by himself at a mountain restaurant, that by the time the concert ended the last train for Klosters would have long since departed, he offered to drive me back. I didn't go, and so never met the girl.

Before I describe the ski pistes and tours available in this area, I must warn you that the experience will not be entirely relaxing, especially on weekends. Swiss skiing is the antithesis of laid-back Sierra skiing. Throngs surge on and off cable cars, many carrying bulky backpacks, nearly trampling the attendants, and there is a fair amount of shoving in lift lines. On the smaller, gondola cars, which accommodate six, an older person will often insist on keeping both windows fully closed and whenever this happens there will invariably be one or more sneezers, coughers, and smokers aboard. I often get off the gondola at the mid-station and wait right there for the next car with an empty seat. Finally, even on advanced pistes watch out for the beginners who seldom make turns, and who are surprisingly numerous in a country where the typical child dons a helmet, boots and skis at the age of three.

You should also be aware that not everyone will welcome your presence. Do not be surprised to be asked why you have come so far to ski when you could have gone to the Rockies instead! (I always answer that I prefer skiing in Switzerland because the vertical drop, at up to six thousand feet, is three times that of most U.S. ski areas.)

From the Gotschnagrat above Klosters there are several challenging runs, both on-piste and off, which lead back to the local network of ski lifts.

Foremost is the Gotschnawang, which is seldom open before February or after early March, and which offers steep powder or mogul skiing (depending on the provenance of the last storm) down to the mid-station of the Gotschnalift. There are *Steilhänge* or cliffs en route; as you face down the piste, work your way over to the left side, across the gully, to minimize the risks, which are considerable.

Next are the two turnoffs from the easy-to-intermediate Casanna run which leads down to the Klosterer *Schwendi*, or mountain restaurant. Drostobel, the first, is the steeper, and rejoins the Casanna *below* the *Schwendi*. Chalbersäss, the second, starts over tundra, continues through woods and ends up with a steep mogul piste which sweeps down to the Casanna just before the *Schwendi*, where a glass of *Glühwein* rewards the intrepid skier. Both of these offer powder when first opened after a storm, and they quickly become 'pisted' by their popularity among expert skiers.

If you continue past the turnoff to the Casanna and its offspring toward the Furka T-bar which initiates access to the higher peaks, you will pass the Seetäli T-bar. As you ride up, you will see first mogul and then powder fields to your left and, at the top, a trail along the ridge to the saddle on your right. Just over the other side begins the *Gemein Böden* (literally, mean ground) off-piste powder run, with variations leading to the middle and valley stations of the Schifer gondola as well as straight down to Klosters.

Last year, as I was making the ten minute climb to the *Gemein Böden*, I saw a helicopter approach and its blades whipped up so much snow that I had to cover my eyes. Seeing this, the pilot withdrew, hovering over a nearby peak, until I had passed. Ahead of me was a couple continuing along the trail; to the left, someone directing the helicopter. As I drew nearer, I finally saw what was occurring: a skier had suffered an apparent heart attack while climbing the trail and was lying motionless on the snow. I asked the couple ahead of me if he was alive and the gentleman replied, casually, in German, 'I doubt it.' The scene still reminds me of the famous Fifth Avenue cameo in the film *Midnight Cowboy*.

The experience also brings to mind a somewhat analogous if less pathetic image of a young girl on crutches trying to negotiate the short stairs leading to a tram exit while the door was closing. Her gratitude when, in the face of indifference by the Zürichoise, I pushed the button to reopen the door expressed itself in a radiant smile which I will never forget.

But I digress. There are several memorable ski tours which begin in one of the two Klosters villages and end up miles away.

Both villages of Klosters border the Silvretta mountain range in Austria, and an off-piste tour from Madrisa to Gargellen and thence, after a thirty-five minute climb with or without skins, down to St. Antönien high above the valley town of Küblis is quite popular. An alternative tour, with virtually no climbing, leads directly over the Rätschenjoch to St. Antönien.

These are also popular hiking routes in summer and autumn, and after taking a postbus from St. Antönien to Pany there is a further hike to Putz, past Lund and Buchen, where you will see the house upon which the above poem is painted, down to Schiers in the valley, whence you return, as from Küblis, by train.

A few minutes above St. Antönien is a mountain restaurant and in the town itself is the Rhätia Hotel, whose restaurant serves a delicious regional specialty similar to ravioli known as Kräpfli, of which there are three kinds: Fleischkräpfli, featuring meat; Chrutkräpfli, made with spinach and cabbage; and Gemischtekräpfli, or a mixture of the first two. The house coffee made with plum brandy and heavy cream and known as *Schümli-Pflümli* is the skier's or hiker's reward for arriving honorably, i.e. by skiing or hiking rather than via the postbus which plies the route between St. Antönien and Küblis.

On the Parsenn range, which has the most reliable and usually the best snow in Switzerland, you can ski down to seven on-piste villages without climbing. In ascending order, these are Küblis, Saas, Klosters, Cavadürli, Wolfgang, Davos Dorf, and Davos Platz, all of which are served by train or postauto or both. The main runs to Klosters have already been described. You can reach Davos directly by skiing one of the trails paralleling the Parsennbahn train tracks, or, more challengingly, by taking the Besenbinder trail below the bottom of the Meierhoftäli T-bar to Wolfgang and then a bus to Davos. The Kulm restaurant in Wolfgang (across the street from the terminus of the ski trial) reserves a private room for Prince Charles and his entourage, whom you may nonetheless spot if you stop there for lunch.

Beyond the beginning of the Hauptertäli *Schlepplift* or T-Bar, under the cable carrying an ancient car over the Strelapass to Schatzalp, you can ski to the small Heimeli restaurant above the high forest town of Sapün. The Heimeli proudly displays a wall-mounted photograph of Prince Charles with his arm around Fritzi, the proprietress.

After a sandwich and beverage, you continue down past the main part of the town and through a forest with attractive views of gorges and frozen waterfalls to Langwies, then take a local train two stops to the ski area of Arosa, board a free bus to the Hörnli lift, and ski down to Tschiertschen, a charming town high above the forested valley leading down to Chur; its best hotel, the Alpina, is located, appropriately, on the ski slope. There are two terraced restaurants in the local ski area. Above it, a further tour over the Jochpass or an unnamed pass further west will take you to the Lenzerheide ski complex, which includes the Rothorn, Weisshorn, Valbella, Parpan and Churwalden lifts. From Valbella, you can cross the road, take the lifts up the Stätzerhorn, and ski down to Domat-Ems, then take a train back to your starting point; or, to complete the circle, from the Lenzerheide Rothorn you can ski through a tunnel to the Promenade and then proceed – again off-piste – on fresh powder down the beautiful valley on the right-hand side directly to the Hörnli lift at Arosa.

There are two main variations on the approach to Langwies. From the Weissfluhgipfel, immediately after exiting the lift and its building, turn left, walk past the overlooking terrace, and put on your skis. (Do not be concerned if aggressive Germans, charging ahead at 9,350 feet above sea level while ignoring the panoramic view of the Jakobshorn and Pischa peaks, the four thousand meter high Piz Bernina in the Engadin and, on the other side of the summit, the Arosa ski area, bump their heads on your skis as you exit the lift. I maul three or four of them a year.) The run ahead of you, which is off-piste, is especially rewarding in spring, when the powder yields to corn snow. You follow the *Spur* or track along the south side of the Gipfel, past three overhanging cliffs and down a mogul field and shallow canyon to the Hauptertäli T-bar, the Strela-

Schatzalp cable car, and, below these, the valley run to Sapün and Langwies.

An alternative run, which begins after a couple of turns to the right, takes you down a steep canyon to a valley from which you can either ski directly to Langwies along the tracks to the left or, preferably with skins, follow the right-hand 'trail' up to the Segnafluh saddle – a two-hour climb – and then ski down fresh powder to Strassberg and along a forest road to Langwies.

From the *north* slope of the Gipfel, again a short way down from the start of the run, there is a turn-off past some cliffs and then a steep descent, known as the Diretissima, down to the Grünsee (a lake) in the valley, whence you can continue (with minimal climbing) over powder fields directly to the bottom station of the Schiferlift or climb over the hill to the left and pick up the variations described in the preceding paragraphs. (Incidentally, the Blockhütte Erezsäss restaurant near the bottom of the Schiferlift offers gourmet stews of veal or venison, sometimes enclosed in a small loaf of bread, and features a succulent roasted half chicken on Saturdays. Its facade bears the heads and antlers of four locally slain stags.)

On your way to the Schiferlift, you will pass a trail which climbs over the Duranna Pass and Fürggli saddle to the Fideris Heuberge ski lift, whence you can ski down to two restaurants facing the afternoon sun and, if conditions permit, on down to Fideris, which smells like the paper factory which is its main feature, or, with additional climbing, further down to Jenaz. Both towns are served by local trains that will take you back to Klosters or Davos.

From Jakobshorn in Davos – where many of the jet set, wearing mirrored sunglasses, congregate during the day – you can ski off-piste on fresh powder to the Dischmatal and Sertigtal valleys, pause at restaurants at the bottom, and then ski back to Davos alongside the track cut for narrower

Langlauf or cross-country skis, or else take a van from either restaurant.

This recitation does not begin to evoke the beauty of the valleys traversed by the off-piste ski runs – most of which take at least an hour – particularly those leading to Sapün above Langwies and to Arosa from the Rothorn. And even the evening runs back to Klosters or Davos offer reflected views of golden sunsets and, in spring, golden valleys.

In summer, this region is equally lovely, if different in mood. There are two decent hotels above the museum in Arosa that are ideally situated for hiking in the surrounding Alpine valleys, the Erzhorn and the Belri. You can walk from the top of the Hörnli down to Tschiertschen or turn left at a junction, climb up to the Promenade and walk down the trail (which begins at the Rothorn above you) to the bottom of the Hörnli lift.

Two other hiking routes to be recommended in these environs are the descent from Schatzalp past the village of Medergen – where in autumn a small restaurant serves *Saft vom Fass*, a mildly alcoholic apple cider from the bottom half of the barrel – to either Langwies or Arosa; and from the Berghaus Vereina high above Klosters down to Süsch or the nearby Flüelastrasse in the lower Engadin. For this latter hike, you can reach the starting point either by walking to the Berghaus or by riding to it in a van operated by the Gotschna Sport shop in Klosters; both are owned by Köbi Boner. An alternative trailhead reached by the van is the Wegerhus on Flüelastrasse. From the terminus of the hike you take a postbus to Davos and a train back to Klosters.

The Flüela pass is itself a lovely drive, as are the Ofen and Albula passes in the Engadin. A few kilometers above La Punt, where the Albula pass begins, is a parking lot and trailhead for a *Höhenweg* (that eventually becomes known as the Via Tarentina) which leads to Zuoz (past a resort hotel and an alpine school) and beyond. The views of the valley, especially in the direction of St. Moritz, are spectacular and unforgettably lovely.

Branching off from Chur is the valley leading to the interconnected Films and Laax ski areas, the latter offering glacier skiing down to the memorable La Ciala piste, which traverses tundra. In late spring, Laax is a rafting center for whitewater trips down the Rhine from Disentis to Ilanz, and there are walking paths along the river in many places e.g., between Bad Ragaz and Landquart.

On the opposite side of the mountains of Flims and Laax, near Lenzerheide, are the mountains of Glarnerland, prominent among them the peak called Karpf. On the other side of Karpf is the ski area of Elm, home of the lemony soft drink Elmer Citro, and on the opposite side of the valley of Elm and a bit further down is the Weissenberg mountain, which is the locus of this digression. From the top of the ski lift, if you climb over the pass and down into the next valley, you will walk past chamois and steinboks through the lovely ski area of Flumserberg all the way to the Walensee, with its subtropical mini-climate and tiny Roman-named towns (Quinten, Quarten) on the opposite shore which are accessible only by boat. Quinten has a pleasant restaurant with an outdoor terrace. If you choose not to take the ferry across, there are local train stops along the near shore at Walenstadt, Murg and Weesen on the Zürich-Chur mainline. If you are driving, Mövenpick's Silberkugel restaurant next to the gas station at the Herrlisberg turnoff (on the eastbound side of the autobahn) features fresh bread, sandwiches, and croissants, and the kiosk where you pay for fuel also stocks the sandwiches, best among which is a pork Wiener schnitzel on a roll.

Another area of Glarnerland which must not be missed is the Klöntal, with the lovely lake called, of course, the Klöntalersee. At the far end of the lake is the tiny town of

Vorauen, with a hotel, two restaurants, a post office and a regular postbus stop. From Vorauen you walk up the beautiful valley, past the Käsernalp restaurant, beyond the high cattle pastures and over a pass to Braunwald, whence a cog railway transports you to the Linthal valley and a postbus returns you to Vorauen. A variant is to take the first postbus beyond Vorauen to Richisau and thus shorten the hike, which the *Wegweiser* or trail signs estimate at eight and a half hours. One gains fourteen hundred meters in altitude as one walks, so this is a hike for the hardy and fit, and one that must be started early in order to arrive in Braunwald by five o'clock or so in time for the train and bus. Except for the absence of high-country lakes, the succession of ever-higher plateaus is reminiscent of the Desolation Wilderness on the western slope of the Sierras.

A word of warning. Hiking in Switzerland is different in three important respects from hiking in, say, the Sierras. You can rarely combine it with swimming, because the lakes both look and are frigid; and at lower elevations in warmer weather the aroma of cow manure will often permeate the air, as it does along the 'Gold Coast' or sunny side of the Lake of Zürich. (Indeed, when the wind is right, the scent even reaches the city proper.) And because the humidity is much higher than in Desolation Wilderness, many savants (especially those older than fifty) delay their hiking at least until the summer heat has broken in mid-August, if not until autumn.

Back to skiing. Further east in Graubünden, over the Julier or Flüela passes, is the Engadin region, of which St. Moritz is the best known village, with its famous café, Hanselmann's, where the specialty of the house is *Schokolade melange*. I prefer Samedan, not far from the glacial ski area of Diavolezza, from the top of which you can ski down either the Val Arlas off-piste powder run or the Morteratsch glacier to the town of that name, take a train back to the ski lift and repeat the run – at least four times in a day, with softer, granular snow on springtime afternoons. Be warned, however, that the glacier is retreating each year as a result of global warming and in the process it is developing additional crevasses, steeper ledges and more precipitous precipices.

(Just beyond Diavolezza is the ski area of Lagalp, beyond which is the Bernina Pass to Poschiavo and Tirano in Italy. In summer and fall, this pass is worth driving over: from Tirano, you continue to Bormio and take the Stelvio pass to the junction (near the Swiss border) with the Umbrailpass, over which you drive through the Swiss National Park down through Santa Maria to Valchava, where the Hotel Central makes a delicious beef filet with a white wine and mushroom sauce. From Valchava you can drive through the valley to Zernez, Susch and Davos, or take the Albula pass at La Punt to Bergun and thence proceed to Davos. In winter, the Albula pass becomes a sled run from its summit to Bergun.)

Between Davos and St. Moritz, on the Engadin side of the Flüela pass but on the north side of the Alps, above the town of Scuol, lies the Tyrolean village of Samnaun, just over the border from the somewhat larger village of Ischgl, Austria, with which it shares a large ski area which is especially popular for its foamy corn snow in spring. The most memorable descent, which leads directly to the heart of Samnaun, is reached from the top of the Palinkopf chair lift on the Austrian side. Of the two roads that converge just outside of Samnaun, the one which passes through Austria is preferable because, unlike the tortuous Swiss road which leads directly to Vinadi and Scuol, its tunnels accommodate two-way traffic. On either road, and in Samnaun itself, there is duty-free shopping for liquor, perfume, clothing and gasoline. You can vary the return trip to Zürich by remaining in Austria and driving through

Landeck, over the Arlberg pass via St. Anton and St. Christoph, and on to St. Gallen and Zürich.

In taking these ski tours, your greatest likelihood of falling is likely to be in the villages you pass through. Even in Klosters, wealthy as it is, the sidewalks remain icy most of the winter, with an occasional handful of dirt thrown on the worst spots. This is so even though the adjacent streets are kept ice-free. The Swiss clearly value property (i.e. automobiles) more than people.

One note of caution: there *is* danger of avalanches; skiers, including their guides, perish every year – twenty in 1997 to date, with numerous additional injuries or lucky escapes. In the event of a mishap, you will not wish to spend the night on the mountain. To minimize the risk, I suggest that you observe these precautions: wait until at least the second day after a storm; go only when temperatures are below the freezing point; avoid touring on heavy, wet snow; take a friend; start early in the morning; when crossing a saddle, choose the shady side if possible; and wear a *Piepser*, or beeper, rentable at many ski shops. But I regularly violate most of these rules, although I do hesitate to go off-piste in warmer weather, and – being somewhat of an *Einzelgänger*, or loner – I generally ski unaccompanied, and without a beeper which, depending on the model, can be heavy to carry. There are many small groups, fathers and daughters, skiing these routes on weekends (especially on Sundays, when the on-piste crowds are the thickest), and the ski schools usually go in midweek, so there are generally others about. But this is not always the case, and being alone in the wilderness, if not the safest experience, can be spiritually satisfying.

Chapter VIII
The Environs of Zürich

Alles OK? Alles klar?
Leder ist Pelz, nur ohne Haar!

Sign in the window of a leather shop in Zürich

During early spring, late autumn and early winter, if there is too little snow for skiing yet too much for hiking in the mountains, one can take a number of enjoyable and scenic forest walks from Zürich to neighboring towns.

There are several informal trailheads. One can begin at Hegibachplatz, climbing up the street of that name, or in Witikon, and follow the signs toward the elegant Degenried restaurant. Or one can trace Klosbachstrasse above Römerhof toward the forest, paralleling the Dolderbahn.

My favorite place to start, however, is at the beginning of the Doldersteig a few blocks above Hottingerplatz. One walks up through a park popular with dog owners toward the Dolder Grand Hotel and the zoo, alongside a river which occasionally stinks from the offal of a pig *Schlachthaus* or slaughterhouse farther upstream. At the first marked junction there is a detour on the right which leads to the Sonnenberg restaurant with its gardens and panoramic views. At the second such junction one can continue toward the zoo and walk past the newly remodeled Zürichberg Hotel, then wander through more woods to the cafeteria above Rigiblick (which is closed on Mondays) and finally traverse the beautiful neighborhood centered around Susenbergstrasse and Freudenbergstrasse on the way back to the Doldersteig. Alternatively, before reaching Rigiplatz, one can cut left down Spyristeig (named after the author of *Heidi*) to Central.

Or, at the second marked junction, one can turn right toward Witikon and Forch, pass a climbable fire tower at Adlisberg, remain in forests high above small villages, follow the yellow trail signs (*Wegweiser*) and blazes through Forch to the Forch Denkmal or monument, at the top of which is a statue symbolizing an eternal flame, and go on to Esslingen, an especially attractive, upscale town. From either Forch or Esslingen one takes the Forchbahn back to Kreuzplatz or Stadelhofen.

The longest of these hikes, to Esslingen, takes about five hours; the others, three and a half to four. One can carry a sandwich and eat at benches along the way or stop in any of the villages for lunch.

An alternative five-hour hike leads past Forch and the expensive Krone restaurant to the Hochwacht observation tower above Pfannenstiel, with panoramic views of the Greifensee (a lake) and the Lake of Zürich. On the way, one passes two mountain restaurants, both with terraces, one of which is the Waldhof in Vorder Guldenen (beyond Forch), which on the day I visited abounded with flies inside. The other, with an outdoor cafeteria and an indoor restaurant, is named after and lies a short walk below the tower in the direction of the town of Pfannenstiel, whose own restaurant offers daily specials, including a succulent lamb stew.

Yet another establishment, the Wassberg hotel-restaurant, lies a ten-minute walk along the trail which branches to the left, a short distance above Ebmatingen, just past the Forch Denkmal. (If when approaching Forch you take the dirt, then paved road straight ahead rather than the trail which branches toward the right, you will walk right past the Wassberg, from which you can also proceed directly to Forch.) This 'Water Mountain' is in fact an excellent watering hole, serving the Ramseier brand of good hard cider to ease the strains of hiking plus a delicious *Tiramisu* to replenish one's energy. In early to mid-November, the weekend specials switch from *coq au vin* and the like to roast goose and goose-liver salad. If your party is large enough, you can order *eine ganze Gans*, a whole goose roasted. The restaurant (which, unlike the hotel, is closed on Wednesdays) features reasonable prices plus scenic views of the Greifensee valley.

If you continue past Forch to Pfannenstiel, because of the spotty bus service it is often necessary to walk for a further hour back to Forch or down to Egg near the Greifensee, or, preferably, along the trail leading past the scenic Bachtobel stream down to the lake of Zürich at Meilen, whence one returns to Zürich by train or (depending upon the hour and season) by steamship. Approaching Meilen, one passes the weekends-only Alpenblick restaurant, which serves cold, hard apple cider. Still closer to town, the trail passes a fine restaurant, the Gasthof zur Burg in the suburb of that name, and then traverses apple and pear orchards plus a couple of impromptu farm stores whose unattended cash boxes are yet another manifestation of the Swiss honor system.

Three variants are also worth mentioning. On the trail to Adlisberg there is a turnoff which leads past Gockhausen and Geeren (site of yet another restaurant) to Stettbach, a town at the end of a tram line which is located about one-third of the way between Zürich and Winterthur and is served by the suburban trains traversing Stadelhofen. Above Stettbach is a notable restaurant, the Wirtschaft Alter Tobelhof, which is closed on Tuesdays and Wednesdays, when you can dine at the somewhat fancier Roter Kamm restaurant two hundred meters below. A few hundred yards before you reach the Tobelhof you cross a trail fork which leads past a pair of sunny benches to Hermikon through Gfenn and around two-thirds of the perimeter of the Dübendorf military airport. Here you can visit an air force museum and, on fine days equally suitable for hiking and flying, watch American fighter jets take off in startlingly close tandem formations. Just before you reach Gfenn, you cross a trail which branches off along a scenic stream toward its source, the Greifensee, and then to the town of that name and Uster. Past the airport, you pass a large humus dump, then walk through a wood and over a hill to Effretikon.

On all of these trails you will see hikers, people with dogs, bikes or both and joggers; but no one sinister. You may pass houses with friendly watchdogs, cats or both, especially between Ebmatingen and Forch.

An alternative hike, equally long but with less climbing, is to take the trail that branches off half a kilometer from the near side of the Wassberg to Zumikon, following the signs to Waltikon and Rehalp, and then walk along the scenic Bachtobel or brook trail to Küsnacht. Along the way, you will see a sign pointing up a short hill to a country restaurant which seems quite popular on weekends; I have yet to try it. After the last Sunday in October, when the steamer service to Meilen ends for the winter, this choice of descent to the lake of Zürich enables the hiker to catch the boat at Küsnacht and proceed either directly or via Erlenbach and Thalwil back to Zürich.

Below the forest, the small, upper-class villages in what is known as 'Zürcher Oberland' are also rewarding to walk through. One can go along dirt paths through Pfaffhausen and Benglen or past schoolchildren walking or riding their bicycles along paved sidewalks and highway underpasses through Ebmatingen and Fällanden to the next lake, the

Greifensee. The path along the left side leads to Uster; on the right, which is the more scenic, to Maur, from which one takes either a bus directly to Zürich or a ferry across the lake to lower Uster, then a bus or further hike to the train station in upper Uster and the train to Stadelhofen or the Zürich main station.

On the other side of the lake of Zürich there is also a complex of hiking trails, centered on the Uetliberg, which is accessible by train and has two restaurants. I prefer to take a train to Bonstetten and then walk over to the next valley and up to the Uetliberg, or else go on to the lovely Sihltal or valley of the Sihl River and take a train back from Sihlbrücke.

From Affoltern, also reached by train, there is an attractive route to the Reuss River and along its shores all the way to Bremgarten. Halfway, on the right-hand side, past a swimming club's private beach which you can nonetheless use in summer, there is a good restaurant; at that point, you should cross the bridge and continue on the left-hand side for the rest of the hike. There is also a decent restaurant on the river at Bremgarten just where you leave the trail to walk up to the train station.

These hikes will extend the off-seasons for skiing and will give you a good workout. When the ski slopes are open, however, you will want to escape from the lake fog of the city and the only slightly less pervasive 'valley' fog of the surrounding regions, which can last with few interruptions from October until May, to the often more cheerful vistas of the Alps.

A further word about the weather in Zürich. As noted, it is almost invariably foggy in cold weather, especially at lake level. You will become grateful for a once-weekly view of the Churpfistern or seven sister peaks beyond the opposite end of the lake. The woods will often be *rauhreif*, coated with hoarfrost. There can be *Hagel* or *Graupel*, which encompass both sleet and hail. (The German word *Eisregen*, which is seldom used in Switzerland, denotes rain which turns to glare ice upon contact with the ground.) Hail in Zürich is as rare as lightning in the Alps during winter, but when it comes the stones can be as large as ice cubes. I have seen such lightning only once, such hail twice, but have often skied or hiked through sleet.

The combination of bleak weather and loneliness can be depressing, especially on the long Christmas and New Year's weekends when virtually everything is closed. There are few tourists with whom to congregate, since virtually all of them are at the ski resorts. Join them.

You will know that spring has arrived when the Knie circus comes to town in May and pitches camp at Sechseläutenplatz near Bellevue for about five weeks (to be followed in early autumn by a competitor and then by shipboard toy and wine expositions).

But it is the summers in Zürich that are most delightful. Since it is often too hot and sticky to hike, everyone swims in the lake, which is one of the cleanest in Switzerland. There is a free beach at the end of Feldeggstrasse, with a kiosk nearby, as well as a number of facilities charging a modest entrance fee, of which the Mythenquai and Tiefenbrunnen bathing areas are the largest. (The former caters to families and retired people, the latter – though it has a shallow swimming pool for toddlers – to singles, with straights on the right and gays on the left, *homo sapiens* vs. *homo erectus*.[1] Also to the left are the grill and cafeteria; the latter offers a phallic popsicle labeled 'The Long One'. Tiefenbrunnen is believed by the straights to be featured in several gay guides to Europe.) There are also the smaller

---

[1] Grandly named Professor Lionel Trilling (born Leonard Cohen) of Columbia, after seeing a male homosexual trounced by a macho character, later confessed that thereafter he never read Wordsworth's line 'The Pansy at my feet' without laughing.

Enge and Utoquai areas which offer a degree of sexual segregation for the religiously conservative, and between which groups of swimmers often traverse the lake during their weekday lunchtimes.

You can meet tourists by riding the lake and river steamers or by lunching at the Bauschänzli restaurant on an island in the Limmat River just shy of the Bellevue Bridge; an added attraction is the interesting view of the Frauenbad, or women's bathing area, where total nudity is common. Further down the lake, toward the Tiefenbrunnen bathing area, are the venerable Fischstube and Zürichhorn Casino restaurants; like the city-operated Rosengarten restaurant at Hottingerplatz and the California restaurant up toward Klusplatz, these offer outdoor terraces for dining.

Two unusual and quite special restaurants in or near Zürich must also be mentioned. Foremost is the Kronenhalle at Bellevue, which has millions of francs worth of Picassos, Miros and the like on display, not always behind glass; your head may rest on a Miro in the main dining room, and even the bathrooms display valuable art. The restaurant's collection was rescued from Germany just before the Nazis took power, and for many years the owner, a *grande dame* who lived into her nineties, would greet guests personally at their tables. *Paté de fois gras* and whole roasted duck – the latter must be ordered at least two hours in advance – are the house specialties; or you can simply choose the *plat du jour* from the rolling cart. Pastries are also chosen in this way.

The second is the Zur Krone at Regensberg, high above the airport, and best reached from Regensdorf: the views upon entering the outskirts of the hilltop town are memorable. The restaurant itself is housed in a sixteenth-century building and the food is succulent.

Two top-drawer cafés are the famous Sprüngli at Paradeplatz and the even better Schober's in the old town across the Limmat River. The specialty of both houses is *Schokolade melange*.

To be avoided are all Chinese restaurants, which are surprisingly expensive and often unsanitary. Many have been exposed for serving soups and foods with unacceptably high counts of coliform bacteria, and I have gotten sick several times at one of the best such establishments in the city.

There is only one Mexican restaurant in Zürich, in the Seefeld area, and I emphatically do not recommend it. Steak fajitas are simply unavailable here, although there is a decent Argentine steak house, the Churasco, in the old town.

Equally unavailable at restaurants are prime ribs of beef on the bone. Mövenpick's Beef Club serves a boneless variety which arrives steamed rather than roasted, lukewarm or cool, and tasteless. My touchstone in this respect is the inimitable Durgin Park restaurant in Boston which serves a twenty ounce slab of beef cooked to perfection and still attached to the entire rib.

Finally, many popular restaurants – e.g. the Zeughauskeller off Paradeplatz – have long-term contracts with Hürlimann beer, which to my taste is the worst in Switzerland, and serve no other brand. A few offer Cardinal or Feldschlösschen, which are better – although the recent merger of the latter with Hürlimann puts its future quality into question. Except for a bar in Stäfa down the lake, there is no place like Tommy's Joint in San Francisco, which serves hundreds of varieties from all over the world. There was a retail outlet near Stadelhofen which offered beers of the world, but it was replaced, sadly, by an Emporio Armani.

Do not be surprised to see well-mannered dogs lying under occupied tables at most restaurants. That is quite legal here, although pets are not permitted in grocery stores or fee-charging swimming areas. Throughout the woods, you will see special garbage containers which dispense doggie bags and their use is the rule, not the exception.

Non-smoking sections in restaurants began to appear about seven years ago and are slowly expanding to more than two tables, but in this respect Switzerland is a far cry from California. Even municipally owned restaurants and concert halls, such as the Opernhaus or Stadttheater, offer only limited havens to those who eschew second-hand tobacco smoke.

While there are no genuine delicatessens in Zürich, there is one close approximation, Bianchi on Marktgasse just off the Limmatquai on the old-town side of the river, which has become an institution. Bianchi supplies all of the city's fine restaurants with shrimp and fish, and has excellent smoked salmon and trout plus U.S. beef at the most reasonable prices in town. On Saturdays after two o'clock, prices for any remaining fresh fish are halved. For the past two years, following a successful lawsuit by nearby residents complaining about the constant smell of fish, the store has been open only on Friday and Saturday except during the week before Christmas, when it reverts to its former six-day-a-week routine. Fowl, fresh fruits and vegetables (try the blood oranges and *kakis* or Japanese persimmons), and an excellent selection of wines are also offered; next door is a top quality bakery offering long loaves of freshly baked bread. The new butcher's shop at Kreuzplatz and the small grocery store at Hottingerplatz also offer an attractive variety of fresh fruits and vegetables.

Zürich has a number of museums, prominent among them the Kunsthaus or art museum, and three major cathedrals, St. Peter's, Grossmünster and Fraumünster; the last has beautiful stained glass windows by Giacometti and Chagall, and there is a postcard concession opposite the latter.

On Tuesday and Friday mornings throughout the year, Bürkliplatz is the site of an outdoor farmers' market where the produce is fresher and (surprisingly) more expensive than in the supermarkets. (I once saw white corn on the cob, or *Maiskolben*, for sale there.) On Saturday mornings, as noted in Chapter Four, the same location features a flea market for which vendors register during the preceding week. As you stroll through the old town and also up to St. Peter's, you will pass additional flea markets and, in warmer weather, food stalls.

Most of the 'A' and virtually all of the 'B' films come to Zürich, and, happily, most of the performances are in English with German and French subtitles, and they typically include amusingly creative advertising, as well as intermissions, which offer an opportunity to purchase low-quality ice cream cones, and which together add about half an hour to the actual screening time. Sometimes an early performance will have harsh German voices dubbed in – except for the Disney movies, for which the studio makes the foreign-language versions, and the songs even rhyme. One of my favorite pastimes is to attend a weekend matinee performance of *Aladdin* or *Pinocchio* in German and watch the children respond so enthusiastically. *Die Schöne und das Biest* (Beauty and the Beast) is even available on CD. In summer, there is an outdoor movie festival on the lake, if you can stand the second-hand cigarette smoke.

As a center of classical music, Zürich is fast improving. The Tonhalle now boasts a top-drawer American music director, David Zinman, formerly of Baltimore and Rochester, who conducts often without benefit of baton and always without the hindrance of stiff collar or tie, and who has so accelerated the orchestra's progression from tenth-rate to first-rate during the past six and a half years that it has achieved comparability with, say, the San Francisco Symphony Orchestra, whose former music director, Herbert Blomstedt, conducted here last season, and it is increasingly attracting top-name soloists.

If you go there, you may be struck by the sight of wives following rather than preceding their husbands into the hall; as often as not, a tall long-legged Swiss male will step into the row, take the nearer of the two reserved seats for which he has purchased tickets and sit down, thus forcing his wife to push past him to the next seat.[2] Once, during a week of city-wide demonstrations on behalf of women's rights, a charming assistant concertmistress, Eiko Furusawa, rose to address the audience before the concert began, and she was so loudly booed and stamped at that her remarks were partially inaudible.

While it is acoustically excellent, the *Grosser Saal* or 'large' auditorium in the Tonhalle is too small to be included on the European tours of many world-class orchestras, although the Vienna Philharmonic makes a biennial appearance. Across the Bellevue Bridge, the opera house is ample for such purposes, but the Zürichoise think that an opera house is only for operas, ballets and orchestral concerts by the resident orchestra, and the hall, though often unused, is never rented to visiting orchestras.[3] Even in these elegant settings, about one-fourth of the time you will encounter aromas that force you to breathe through your mouth, and you may remember with nostalgia the old *Dial* soap ads which appeared in New York subway trains a couple of decades ago: 'Aren't you glad you use *Dial* soap? Don't you wish everybody did?'[4]

---

[2] The obese concertmaster of the deservedly less renowned Zürich *Kammerorchester* (Chamber Orchestra) invariably exhibits this discourtesy towards his female colleagues in the string section.

[3] With regard to opera and concert tickets, be advised that the word *frei* means available, not free of charge, for which the German word is *gratis*.

[4] I am reminded of Antony's admonition to the Roman citizens in Shakespeare's *Julius Caesar*: 'Nay, press not so upon me; stand far off.'

Chapter IX
Goods and Services

The quality of goods and services in Switzerland is nonpareil. Take Swissair when you come – if you dare[1]. Ask the flight attendant for a drink. She will immediately and cheerfully bring you one instead of admonishing you that you will have to wait until the cart comes around. There will be no lectures about the duties incumbent upon anyone sitting next to an emergency exit. If you are in first or business class, the attendant will volunteer to hang up your coat, rather than demur because the closet is rapidly filling up and half the section hasn't boarded yet. In short, there is no hassle and you will seldom if ever be treated as less important or less valued than your neighbor in the same class of service. Delta, are you paying attention?

Service on your automobile will be done perfectly the first time, although you may have to wait a couple of days for parts to be located, ordered and shipped. There is virtually no aftermarket in Switzerland; if you need windshield wipers or an outside mirror for a Honda you must obtain them from a Honda *Vertretung*, or dealer.

Switzerland is a country in perpetual mourning, or at least it appears so from the national predilection for wearing black. Many Swiss think that black is the only decent color and they wear black business suits and dresses, sometimes

---

[1] Please see my forthcoming book on the airline industry, *Contrails and Entrails*.

called 'charcoal'; black skis and ski suits; black bikinis; black tights and leotards; even black T-shirts, jeans and leather jackets. A typical young Swiss woman wearing a black sweater, black miniskirt, black tights and pumps, guiding a black dog with one hand and, increasingly, an African boyfriend with the other looks exactly like a Parisian *poule*, as timelessly described by Hemingway in *The Sun Also Rises*, only with better teeth – and, one hopes, more interesting conversation. The color black really does predominate. Red (Stendhal) is somewhat less common. But ski suits of pink, purple and lavender hues are worn without embarrassment by the most macho youths. Ditto green, a very popular color for sports jackets, ties and ski suits. You can usually find all violet or purple and green ski gloves at reduced prices.

Yet the upper classes, whom you encounter at private banks, fine restaurants and concerts, do seem to prefer navy blue. At many elegant gatherings this is the universal color, and it usually is worn solid, without pinstripes. That gentleman in front of you with the bold chalk pinstripes is undoubtedly British.

All of this is by way of preamble to some shopping tips. Note at the start that shops close at six-thirty in the evening during the week and at four in the afternoon on Saturday, and are closed on Sundays and holidays. The exceptions to this are the Bahnhofstrasse shops which remain open on Thursday nights until eight-thirty; the stores in the Stadelhofen station which are open on Sunday afternoons; and the shops in the main station and at the airport which seem always to be open.

If you want a good raincoat, you can buy Burberry's during the biannual sales for roughly what you would pay in the U.S.: Weinberg's elegant store on the Bahnhofstrasse in Zürich, as well as Day's across the street, sells them then for half price, or roughly six hundred Swiss francs.

Aquascutum's, which I find superior by virtue of their all cotton shells and all wool linings to Burberry's polyester blends, are more reasonably priced in the U.S. (and, no doubt, in London as well). At the Aquascutum store on Beacon Street in Boston one can find a coat with zip-out lining in the fashionable below-the-knees European length for $ 439 on sale, reduced from $ 639, and the models with buttoned linings cost about one hundred dollars less. At London House in Zürich, a few doors from Day's, the zipper model costs twelve hundred Swiss francs, and I have never seen it reduced; a single outsized coat without a wool lining was marked down by only thirty percent, to seven hundred Swiss francs.

Until March, 1997, if one was looking for a new suit – I refer here to male customers, as I know nothing about women's fashions – one of the best shops to visit in Zürich was Fritz Hägi's boutique on Feldeggstrasse, between Kreuzplatz and Mühlebachstrasse. Near the end of that month, at the age of seventy-one, after twenty-five years of serving the city's elite, Mr. Hägi closed the shop and retired. He claimed that the recession in retail sales had nothing to do with his decision; his wife privately disagreed, noting that many of their customers had lost their jobs. Merchandise *did* seem to move somewhat more briskly after the couple inaugurated a fifty percent-off, total liquidation sale in September, 1996.

Herr Hägi would show you fabrics from England identical to those proffered by the best tailors on Savile Row, including (for sports jackets) a fantastic silk and wool mixture, and he would recommend items if you asked. His taste was invariably excellent, his wife's even better. Once you gave the word – no deposit, just your word – the material would be ordered, cut, lined and tailored, all in three weeks' time. It always fitted perfectly, was monogrammed with your initials on the lining, was *fully* lined (including the trousers, to protect the knees) and it would further both your career and image, at a cost of roughly nine hundred to thirteen hundred Swiss francs. The shop stocked tastefully chosen, ready-made casual jackets of wool and acrylic, also lined; unlined cashmere jackets and merino wool sweaters; sports jackets; cashmere overcoats (two thousand, five hundred Swiss francs); small leather goods; and accessories. Unlike many local shop owners, Herr Hägi did not order all or even most of his ready-made jackets in the widest shoulder size so that you never looked, as many mid-level Swiss bank employees do, as though both shoulders of your jacket needed to be reduced.

Now that this corner of elegance has passed into history, the best places to go are the expensive London House store on Bahnhofstrasse or the Bovet shop on Talacker; or, at a more reasonable price level, the New Yorker shop next door to Bovet; or the flagship Spengler store on Sihlstrasse; or Orville Mode on Stockerstrasse (ask for the owner, Mr. Mossbacher, to serve you personally). There are cheaper shops as well, some of them frequented by well-to-do bankers – e.g. Bernie's on the Niederdorfstrasse – but they can generally be characterized as offering what New Yorkers call 'schlock' merchandise, and I would avoid them.

As distinguished from blazers, the Swiss generally recognize only one pattern for a sports jacket: houndstooth checks. You can find small, medium and large checks; but other patterns, such as plaids, simply don't exist. This holds true even for Brioni jackets, and characterized most of Herr Hägi's samples as well.

A bit of definition: a *Veston* is a suit coat or sports coat, and both can also be called a *Jacke*, or jacket, as is a cardigan cashmere sweater that covers your hips, or a leather jacket (but not a full-length one which is a *Mantel*, or coat). What we call a vest, sleeveless, is a *Weste* or *Gilet*. *Hosen* are trousers, not socks, which are *Socken*, and which come in varying lengths but never with garters. The High German word for tie which you may have learned at university, *Schlips*, is understood to mean T-shirt in Switzerland; a tie is always referred to as a *Kravatte*. If you order your custom-made suit *feinmass*, i.e. perfectly measured and tailored – as opposed to one that is a *Masskonfektion*, or ready-made with custom alterations – the coat will probably have sleeve buttons at the cuffs which actually function. To show people that your suit is expensive, you must leave one or more of these buttons undone. Vanity, vanity, all is vanity.

Except at Globus, where most young Swiss bank clerks buy zoot suits for four hundred Swiss francs, the typical store does not stock more than one size of each item so that the suit you see in a window may well not be available in your size. This was sometimes true even at Herr Hägi's boutique, but he would gladly and quickly obtain your size. Average inventory for a boutique or small store is only about ten thousand Swiss francs. Switzerland is a shortage society, not geared to instant gratification. When you see a ready-made item that you like in your size, seize it. *Carpe diem* applies to shopping here as well as to skiing.

Shirts and shoes, however, are another story. Perhaps you read all of *Gulliver's Travels* as a child, not just his adventures in Lilliput. If so, you may remember the ingenious if flawed method of measuring clothes practiced in the egghead kingdom of Laputa. The only measurement taken by a Laputan tailor was the circumference of the thumb. Doubling this, he deduced the size of the wrist and, by similar geometric progression, the other relevant measurements.

Well, the Swiss think that your collar size is proportionate to your arm length, or vice versa. There is only one sleeve length per neck size and only one collar circumference per sleeve size in ready-made shirts. If you happen not to match the theoretical symmetry of the Laputans, or if you wish a tapered shirt or 'body' shirt, you must order a quantity from a custom shirtmaker. I recommend Classic House on the wide alley called Im Gasse off Paradeplatz in Zürich. The Swiss think in decimals, rather than duodecimals, so the affable owners of Classic House, the Von Gleichens, will offer you an eleventh shirt free if you order ten. If you are at all like me, however, you will want a full dozen shirts, not eleven, so order eleven and get the twelfth one free. For my dozen shirts of white or ecru broadcloth or blue fils-à-fils, I pay fourteen hundred and thirty Swiss francs, or just under one hundred and twenty Swiss francs per shirt, which is less than many ready-made shirts cost; and, unlike ready-mades, they look and feel tailored. (There are also Classic Houses in Kilchberg and St. Moritz.)

Happily, all colors and patterns of dress shirts – and ties – are acceptable here, at least during working hours; short sleeves are common in summer and jackets are often carried or left in one's office. At concerts, however, long-sleeved white shirts do predominate. In this respect, Zürich is much more like a coastal American city than a southern or Midwestern one like Cincinnati, where Procter & Gamble's conservative influence has resulted in a ninety-nine percent acceptance of long-sleeved white shirts all year round, even on summer days when the mercury hovers near or above one hundred degrees Fahrenheit, and where office workers never visit each other without wearing their jackets.

Although women's shoes come in widths, men's generally don't; the private Bally shoe and luggage store near Paradeplatz is an exception. Usually only the widest width is available, sometimes the next to widest as well, and the clerk will attempt to compensate by downsizing the length and inserting an insole. Oddly, the toes, especially on Italian shoes, are too narrow. Reject this compromise, as your feet will develop corns and be generally uncomfortable. Instead, either bring shoes with you upon returning from visits to the U.S. or order Church shoes from the Jermyn Street shop in London. But beware: British sizes are different. In general, you go out two widths and down one length, so that a 10B, for example, is a 9D. But it can also be a 9.5D, or a 9E or 9.5E, depending upon the last. (In Swiss sizes, it will be either a 42.5 or a 43.) In any case, the British will remit their value added tax when charging your credit card, and they will mail the shoes to you in Switzerland. A week or so thereafter, the post office will send you a notice to collect your package, and you will have to pay the Swiss value added tax. All told, you will end up paying a price about midway between full U.S. retail and the twice a year sale level, and well below the prevailing Swiss level.

Hiking, ski and after-ski boots, however, do come in various widths, and you can be fitted comfortably in any sports shop. Whereas you should buy ski boots at a resort shop – often you can exchange them after a day for a more comfortable model – hiking boots are best purchased at half-price in January at Gräb on Oberdorfstrasse in Zürich. On a Saturday afternoon, half the town seems to be there. While the most expensive models are not reduced, the shop has excellent inventory. I recommend Raichle hiking boots, made in Switzerland;[2] the three top leather models, in ascending order of stiffness and tread depth, are the Julier, Oberalp and Mountain Trekker. You should avoid the Goretex varieties, as they are simply too hot for most hiking weather. If you have wide feet, you may prefer the German

---

[2]Raichle is now owned by Dachstein of Austria, and its products have become less available outside of Zürich, even in cantons bordering Austria; the German brands have filled the partial vacuum.

brands Löwa or Meindl. In most brands, the stiffer models will require two pairs of socks, at least initially. For after-ski boots, Kandahar is the best available here, or you can obtain Blondo models in the U.S., Canada or England. Avoid Salomon hiking boots as well as modified jogging shoes with deeper treads as they offer neither sufficient arch support nor heel and toe protection from sharp rocks.

If you do find yourself in need of a new pair of hiking boots while in a mountain resort, the sports shops can, of course, accommodate you. In Zermatt, Burgener has a full selection of Raichle and other brands; in Klosters, I recommend Andrist Sport shop.

You needn't bring toiletries and cosmetics from America. The brands here are superior. I recommend Nivea cream soap (which no longer comes in a bath size) and Bac stick deodorant, both of which are available cheaply at the Coop supermarket, as well as Ambre Solaire or the upscale Vichy sun creams, which won't run in your eyes like Coppertone and Shade products by Schering-Plough. Vichy also makes a mild, non-allergenic deodorant. Excellent lip pomades are made by Roc, Bepanthol, and Ilrido. You will find Chesebrough vaseline, Alcon artificial tears, Gaviscon antacid tablets, Colgate toothpastes, Neutrogena shampoos, Dove and Lux soaps, and Nivea lotions (which originated in Europe) readily available, though usually in very small sizes – about two and six-tenths ounces for Colgate, less than half an ounce for artificial tears: the Swiss will solemnly assure you that once the tiny bottle is opened, it must be used up within a month to avoid contamination by bacteria.

Because product line upgrades are unusually rapid here, you should avoid becoming attached to a particular brand, especially of shampoo. Simple, mild varieties for frequent use are regularly discontinued. Since I have lived here, Neutrogena, Guhl and L'Oreal's Phyto Kyr have all followed this pattern, abandoning this segment of the market to Klorane and Rausch.

When you buy a ski suit, the shopkeeper will encourage you to have it dry cleaned at least half the time. Ignore her, and wash it in mild detergent and warm water, as it will last far longer if you do. Avoid having your skis serviced more than twice a season as the shops grind them down excessively so that you will have to buy a new pair, and the technology is not so advanced as, say, Squaw Valley's. Indeed, many ski shops hand out three coupons, each valid for a fifty-franc service, in order to encourage frequent 'tune-ups'.

If you want to buy a grill pan for cooking steaks in the broiler-oven – which (in a modern Electrolux) gives you the option of using both upper and lower elements for broiling and baking simultaneously – the clerk will try to sell you an electric grill or a microwave oven. Be wary.

A word about coin-operated machines which dispense stamps, gasoline or snacks. The post office's outside vending units do not give change or return any coins you deposit; after a couple of minutes, if you fail to press the right buttons, you will automatically receive a stamp equal in value to the amount deposited. Similarly, gasoline dispensers will issue a receipt if you foul up, and you have to mail it to the station in order to get a refund. Snack machines at train stations will refund only a small portion of what you deposit; once you drop, say, a five-franc piece, you *must* buy something, or the next customer will be able to take advantage of your generosity.

A word about books and magazines. There are a few bookstores which sell English-language books, the best being Staeheli's on Zürich's Bahnhofstrasse. Prices are somewhat higher than their U.S. dollar counterparts and it can take weeks for an ordered book to arrive. *The Wall Street Journal, Financial Times, The Economist, International Herald*

Tribune, Time and *Newsweek* are available at newsstands, but not, sadly, the *New Yorker* magazine, in which (as in *Time, Newsweek* and the *Financial Times*) Minerva Press advertises.

Finally, a word about Swiss wines. There are excellent white wines, among them Epesse and Yvorne, and the Clos des Abbayes brand of Dezaley, from Lausanne. The latter does not travel well and must be drunk immediately upon being uncorked as the delicate bouquet quickly evaporates and the wine then essentially degenerates into an ordinary Chablis. My favorite local red wine is Pinot Noir; the best varieties possess the softness of a good French Beaune. And the French wines, of course, continue to set the standard. Compare any Swiss white wine against a good Sancerre or Meursault Charmes, and you will serve the latter to your best company.

Postscript
Slumming Among the Swiss

Alles vergängliche ist nur ein Gleichnis.
Das unzulängliche hier wird's Ereignis.
Das unbeschreibliche hier ist's getan.
Das ewig weibliche zieht uns hinan.

The past is prelude.
The unattainable becomes actual.
The indescribable is invested with form.
The eternal feminine impels us onward.

Goethe

Before every meal – even a sandwich eaten while sitting on a rock along a mountain trail – the Swiss wish you 'good appetite', which in the Germanic dialects is *En guete* or, more often, simply *guete*. When I first arrived, I misunderstood the pronunciation and thought that the Swiss invariably invoked the poet Goethe before digging into a meal so I would respond, to much puzzlement, by quoting the above epigraph, which comprises the last four lines of *Faust*, and which otherwise has nothing to do with the rest of this chapter, for which a more fitting introduction would be Jake's ditty in Hemingway's *The Sun Also Rises*, which I always imagine being sung to the tune of 'The Bells are Ringing':

O give me irony,
And give me pity.
O give me irony,
When you're feeling [shitty].

You may have formed the impression that I love Switzerland but am ambivalent about the Swiss. If so, you are right. There are positives and negatives, as in any country, and I summarize these below. But I seem to be left with a bad taste in my mouth more often than elsewhere.

Of course, my perceptions are no doubt biased by the difficulties I have experienced in staying employed here, which I have adumbrated at various points throughout the preceding chapters. It probably will not surprise you to learn that I have spent much of the past four years enjoying the ski tours and hiking adventures that I have been describing while intermittently searching for a new position. Living well is the best revenge; I cannot deny a certain pleasure in the recurrent thought that the Swiss who keep refusing to hire me are in the meantime sitting in their offices in foggy Zürich and playing their little power games. Many of them are well aware and quite naturally resentful of my current activities in the sunny Alps – activities which are far more pleasant than staying at home and waiting for the telephone to ring, which it rarely does, or for the postman to bring good news, which never comes.

The excuses they give are virtually random. Examples: 'Your résumé does not correspond to our profile requirements in all respects.' (Translation: 'You are too old.') 'We don't hire part-time or freelance employees.' (Who said anything about either of these categories? Certainly not I.) 'You are a front office person, and this is a back office job.' (As an analyst, I have only rarely met with clients or spoken with them on the telephone.) Or the catch-all 'explanation': 'We need someone who speaks Swiss-German.' (Why?)

But the Swiss are invariably polite in their letters of refusal, in which they generally return my résumé and references, and they always close by wishing me success in my future endeavors; the French-Swiss in Geneva add their distinguished salutations. Most letters also mention that no suitable position is available. On one occasion, I persisted and asked to be considered for *any* position; the reply maintained politeness while subtly changing the formula to indicate that there was no position for which I was suitable. Only once did I press an otherwise gentlemanly respondent to the point of exasperation, to my continuing regret.

Corresponding letters from American firms that I have approached are not always so polite. One writer advised me to realize that I was competing with highly qualified applicants for a position as a healthcare analyst. (I took this to mean that some of my competitors were not only certified financial analysts but also had completed doctorates in biochemistry.) Another writer sarcastically expressed his hope that I could find a position in the investment business. Two others wrote that they only hire, in one case, persons no older than thirty-three, in the other, 'fresh talent' rather than 'experienced veterans' or 'old dogs'. When I quickly dispatched letters of protest to both firms, the first stubbornly restated its age bias, while the second ignored me altogether.

At the same time, upon receiving these letters, I immediately filed discrimination charges with the U.S. Equal Employment Opportunity Commission against both firms, which subsequently invited me to interviews for which I footed most of the travel expenses. Not surprisingly, neither interview resulted in a job offer, but rather in a repeated denial of my application.

In the first case, which involved the Swiss office of a prominent U.S. firm headquartered in Manhattan, the New York City regional office of the EEOC subpoenaed the résumés of recent applicants in order to determine their average ages, and was flooded with scores of documents, mostly in German. Having digested these, and determined that no one over the age of thirty-three had indeed been hired during the calendar year in question, the Commission sought further information under subpoena as to the number of older Americans whom this office had declined to employ in the past. If the figure were large enough, the government intended to exercise its right to litigate the substantial issues involved, probably via a class action – in which event the case would hit the press, I would become famous, and my chances of finding a job would diminish even further.

Meanwhile, active negotiations between the firm and me were in progress, but these were suspended when the EEOC notified the respondent that it was not prepared to honor a private settlement until the company provided the additional information it sought.

A month later, however, in October, 1996, after pursuing its demographic research, the EEOC determined that the number of Americans engaged in the profession in question was too small to justify bringing its resources to bear, and it agreed to honor the agreement that had been tentatively negotiated. The prospect of poring over additional truckloads of documents written in German was also daunting, one official confessed, and the legal department was not confident it could prove that I would have been hired but for my age.

The Commission then duly issued a 'determination' (reproduced in the Appendix) finding the firm guilty of having violated the age discrimination provisions of civil rights law, and formulated a 'conciliation agreement' calling for the firm to compensate me in lieu of facing a lawsuit. I received a copy of the former – which would be crucial evidence if, in the absence of a settlement, I were to file a private lawsuit within six months of receiving it – and I was subsequently sent the latter for my signature. The investigator first hinted that it would contain a pleasant surprise: a level of compensation (payable in U.S. dollars by certified check) substantially above what I had negotiated with the offending company's attorney, for whom I was no match. But this pipe dream was dispelled by the government's attorney, who was not prepared to support a larger settlement, given his doubts about my qualifications relative to those of other applicants. The appreciation of the U.S. dollar against the Swiss franc, however, effectively added a bonus to the amount specified by the document as the minimum settlement acceptable to the EEOC's regional director, and therefore to me.

The eventual agreement also required the firm to submit to the Commission for the next two years semiannual reports listing all job applicants covered by the Age Discrimination in Employment Act (ADEA), i.e. U.S. citizens over forty and under seventy – by name, age, sex, and nationality, identifying those hired and tallying the number of new hires who are forty or older. Although the Zürich office hires only three percent of all applicants, this seemingly draconian measure actually will impose only a modicum of paperwork since only a handful of the job-seekers are Americans. But during the same two years the company will also be constrained to post a notice, visible to current staff and applicants alike, stating that it is an equal opportunity employer and inviting disgruntled persons to contact the U.S. Equal Employment Opportunity Commission at the address provided in the notice![1]

I suspect that such onerous provisions would have attracted the remedial attention of the now-defunct Council on Economic Competitiveness which was founded and headed by Dan Quayle. But after more than three years of being pushed around by corporate personnel departments in Zürich, I do experience a great satisfaction in causing a local company of critical mass to be hobbled in a way that promises not only to be beneficial to future job-seekers other than myself – as a condition of settlement I had to agree not to apply for a position with the firm in the future – but quite humiliating as well. Vengeance is mine, saith the Lord.

A word about the EEOC's senior investigator assigned to this case, Mrs. Elizabeth Singletary, is in order. While Johnny Cochran, O.J. Simpson's lead defense counsel in the criminal trial, took umbrage at the notion that there is such a thing as a recognizable black accent or voice, I beg to differ. As a former college instructor of language and literature who has lived abroad for a fairly long time, I am confident that the investigator is a highly cultivated, infallibly courteous and pleasant black woman who has an incredible work ethic. I know that she is at her desk by eight, generally eats a homemade sandwich for lunch there, and remains until 6:30 p.m.; that she has worked at the agency for the past twenty-eight years; and that she enjoys, to use her own words, 'going for the jugular' when it comes to imposing sanctions upon a corporate offender.

This particular case, in which a formerly well-paid financial analyst located in Switzerland and a top-drawer

---

[1]Whether or how the E.E.O.C. will verify compliance with this requirement is unclear The investigator expressed willingness to travel to Zürich for this purpose. After twenty-eight years of dedicated service (see below), surely she deserves such a field trip at taxpayers' expense.

American attorney accustomed to stratospheric levels of income alternated in calling her several times a week to seek counsel, obtain information or court approval, was clearly a gratifying highlight of her career. Within her domain, she has considerable power: she made us wait and then go forward at her pace, and she waived such arcane Commission rules as that payment of the settlement must be made by certified check – a virtually unknown instrument in Switzerland, where all parties to the dispute preferred the transaction to be made in the local currency. In anticipation of Christmas week, which she planned to spend at home, she brought the necessary computer disk from the office, gave us her private telephone number, and waited until I called her, then patched in the attorney so that we could all confer together. Her pride in her professionalism is both evident and well-founded, and I salute her.

My respect for Mrs. Singletary increased further when I accidentally learned that she wears leg braces as a result of a 1995 accident in which the elevator at her place of employment plunged four floors. Although she eventually located an attorney who filed suit on a contingency-fee basis, she has yet to collect any compensation. During her year of recuperation she was forced to use up her accumulated leave, and she was not even granted a supervisor's privilege of remote retrieval of voice-mail messages left at the office.

It took four months for the lawyers representing the company and the government to haggle over the fine print. 'The devil', said the eminent outside attorney retained by the firm, 'is in the details', which is a felicitous if trite expression that I had not previously encountered. Notwithstanding the notice, described five paragraphs above, in settling my claim I had to promise to disclose neither the name of the firm nor the terms of the agreement lest hordes of older American job-seekers apply and upon rejection sue the company. The inclusion of such a non-disclosure clause shields an EEOC case settled privately (i.e. without litigation) from anyone seeking to discover its documentation by invoking the Freedom of Information Act. Only the IRS will be made privy to the details.

At the end of February, 1997, I finally received the funds called for in the settlement, with a 'bonus' provided by the fourteen percent appreciation of the U.S. dollar relative to the Swiss franc since the settlement was negotiated four months previously. On 1st March I finally began to enjoy an unusually good ski season in Klosters and (for two weeks) Zermatt.

The tax implications of my settlement are in fact rather unusual, both in Switzerland and in the United States. While the double taxation treaty between the two countries which took effect at the beginning of 1996 will protect me from being assessed twice, it was not immediately obvious which jurisdiction could assert liability.

Since I neither worked for the firm in question nor was authorized to do so, it would be illegal for my name to appear on its Swiss payroll. Indeed, the parent corporation, domiciled in the U.S., has indicated that no report of the transaction will be made to the Swiss authorities even though I was paid in Swiss francs in Switzerland by direct deposit to a Swiss bank account from its Swiss subsidiary's funds at a time when my actual and legal residence was in Switzerland. Thus according to two senior tax advisers at a major bank here, the settlement will not constitute Swiss income, and it is not taxable as such.

Clearly, the source of the funds is American: without U.S. law, or if I were not myself a U.S. citizen, I would have had no case in the first place. The negotiations were exclusively with the parent corporation, which has stated its intention of reporting the payment to the Internal Revenue Service via a 1099 form. But no U.S. taxes were withheld and, from an American viewpoint, according to an experienced U.S. accountant, the settlement will constitute earned income from a foreign source and it therefore will qualify for the foreign earned income exemption. Of course, if there are no related Swiss taxes, there will be no foreign tax credit to offset any U.S. tax liability on the unsheltered portion. But I will not have to file any quarterly estimated return along with an appropriate payment, because I had no U.S. tax liability in the preceding year.

There is another, more sobering aspect to this entire matter: the putative status of the unfortunate personnel official who sent me the two letters expressing illegal age discrimination. Having experienced unemployment, I can only hope that the firm does not treat her as a scapegoat for its own illegal actions and policies, but I am not optimistic about her job stability there.

In the second case, which was settled for a modest sum (from which U.S. taxes *were* withheld) in March, 1997, the position had not then been filled, according to the personnel department. I was skeptical of this assertion, however, because brokers had identified a young analyst performing the duties I had contemplated, and since the industry's annual directory, for which the cutoff date was 10th June, 1996, lists a new member of the firm with precisely the specialties and functions for which I had applied, and for which the firm was allegedly seeking to hire someone. (Because this person has Roman numerals after his surname, I shall refer to him as 'Row, Row, Row'.) I also found suspect the claim that the person to whom I originally applied (whom I think of by the ducky appellation of Base Canard Junior because of his unusual given name) is not involved in the hiring process: in 1996 the same directory listed him as an investment firm manager, and the 1997 edition indicates that he is a chief investment officer. Moreover, his letter makes clear that he was actively involved in both the decision to hire a full-time director of research and in the choice of the successful candidate in 1995. At any rate, now that the case has been settled, the firm is free to hire a comparatively young applicant, even someone over forty – if in fact it wishes to fill the position – without the risk of strengthening my claim. Six months after the case was settled I received a letter from the Massachusetts Human Rights Commission notifying me that it was also closing the case in light of the outcome of the EEOC case. Until I received this letter, I hadn't even known that the state commission was involved in the matter.

The EEOC's jurisdiction in both cases derived under Title VII of the Civil Rights Act of 1964 and its subsequent amendments. This legislation explicitly extends to Americans discriminated against by wholly owned and managed foreign subsidiaries of U.S. firms, even in countries which have no laws against age, sex, ethnic or religious discrimination. This is a valuable protection, since no foreign country I know of enforces such a policy. (Prime Minister Tony Blair has promised to introduce such legislation in the U.K.)

I negotiated both settlements without the benefit of an attorney, since I was unable to find one willing to take a stake in either of my claims on a contingency basis and since the respondent's attorneys were from high-powered firms against which few plaintiffs or their attorneys could afford to compete or even attempt to outbluff or outmaneuver. While awaiting the final settlements, I read three books that collectively document this all too common predicament: Ralph Nader's *No Contest*, Robert Grafton's *Making Elite Lawyers*, and Sol Linowitz's elegantly written *The Betrayed Profession*.

In the meantime, I have continued my job search both in Switzerland and (notwithstanding the logistical obstacles) in the United States. Unfortunately, there is a widespread bias among American businessmen that anyone who emigrated abroad, especially to a non-English-speaking country, must be incompetent or unpatriotic or both; and indeed, the image of Swiss secondary schools and medical colleges as institutions of last resort tends to reinforce this prejudice. The few U.S. businessmen who value foreign experience seek expertise in overseas markets, which outside of the healthcare industry I cannot offer.

When I initially wrote this section in September, 1996, having been turned down as a candidate for two positions as an editor of English manuscripts and a translator of German and French texts, I was theoretically facing expulsion from Switzerland by the end of the year, unless one of my still pending job applications were to bear fruit. It is frustrating that I was turned down for both translation positions solely on the basis of age, despite performing well in two test translations, one of which was without benefit of a dictionary.

In early October, I learned from Herr Hägi that there is an ombudsman for such problems. I looked in the telephone book and it turns out that there are several, including one for the city of Zürich and one for the canton. Naturally, I was obliged to make appointments with both: the *Arbeitsamt*, or employment office, is a metropolitan agency, while the *Fremdenpolizei* or 'foreigners' police' are cantonal. The conversations were free of charge, and it even appears that the two ombudsmen may actually have consulted with each other about my problem, but their letters and telephone calls to the authorities were of no avail.

Regarding a 'C' permit, the foreigners' police took the hardest possible line, insisting on the requirement that one must work for five uninterrupted years in order to qualify. I suspect their answer might have been more favorable had I not accepted the unemployment compensation. My upstairs neighbor, a professor of law, was granted a 'C' permit as soon as she arrived to begin teaching at the university, but that is owned by the city, and she is German.

The option to declare *Selbständigkeit*, accept freelance assignments (which abound) and tap into one's pension money is open only to Swiss citizens or to holders of a Type 'C' permit, which (since I originally came here to work under a 'B' permit) I can eventually obtain only by winning a secure, full-time, long-lasting position. This 'Catch-22' situation is called *ein Teufelskreis*, a devil's circle, by the Swiss.

In their letter, the foreigners' police warned that they would soon give me a deadline for leaving the canton which, practically speaking, means the country. Three weeks later they did so, establishing 30th December as the cutoff date, and giving me twenty days to appeal their decision.

At the time, this edict felt like a death sentence, especially when I contemplated losing my financial independence and returning to my birthplace of Cincinnati, that reactionary, racially tense and provincial 'Queen City' settled by Germans, with its seven 'Teutonic' brands of weak local beer, its high crime rate (especially in the 'Over the Rhine' neighborhood a few blocks north of downtown), its carcinogenic atmosphere, oppressive weather, pollinated air and polluted drinking water, and overheated swimming pools. In the 1950s, Marie Wilson, the amply endowed blonde actress who starred in *My Friend Irma*, shocked playgoers by appearing in one scene wrapped in a towel without her 'stays'; in the 1960s, a young female colleague of hometown boy Jerry Rubin (together with his less well-known brother Gilbert, a wealthy orphan) was beaten with umbrellas by outraged matrons after she protested during a political rally by stripping off all her clothes; and even in the mid-1990s, the card catalogue of the main branch of the public library in Cincinnati lists Karen Salmansohn's provocative book *How to Succeed in Business Without a Penis* by omitting the last two letters of the ultimate word in the title; and a memorable line in the play *Sylvia*, in which an attractive, young, and feisty woman plays, literally, a bitch, could still produce shocked gasps in the audience: 'Look at the balls on that Dalmatian!'

Cincinnati is still one of those places where people tend to remain children all their lives, parroting and transmitting the values inculcated in them by their parents, adopting their father's (or father-in-law's) profession or business[2] and joining one or more parochial country clubs which, like the city's ethnically segregated neighborhoods or the high school fraternities and sororities sponsored by the Board of Education, are designed to limit their social contacts to persons from comparable social and religious backgrounds. When they grow up, they aspire to such offices as the presidency of the local ethnic cemetery. The high-school classmates whom I considered interesting intermarried soon after graduation and moved away. Two of the young women landed in Zürich and Lucerne, and our notable alumni included James Levine, Steven Spielberg and Jim Dine.[3]

---

[2]An acquaintance of mine who wished to be a musician or teacher but whose father, a physician, pressured him to study medicine, resolved the intolerable conflict by committing suicide. The conservative daily newspaper ran the story under the headline, 'Fall Kills Amberley Resident', while its more liberal competition screamed 'Doctor's Son Leaps To Death!'

[3]In the 1950s, in either Sabina or Medina, both small towns north of Cincinnati, there was still exhibited in a central square the embalmed corpse of 'Clarence', an unidentified black man found lying dead by the roadside during the depression of the 1930s. The stated purpose of the

Thankfully, the appeals process – which could postpone if not ultimately preclude this fate – turned out to be comparatively liberal and the deadline not to be graven in stone. A week after receiving the *Fremdenpolizei's* ultimatum, I telephoned their office, and was informed by the head of the department that if I had a position in prospect but not yet fully contracted toward the end of the grace period, I could obtain an extension of several months simply by informing them of this via registered letter. Conversely, if I were to leave by the deadline, their order to do so would take precedence over the provision of my apartment lease that requires me to give the owner three months' notice of intention to vacate the premises; but I would be liable for rent after that date. Since I did have pending job applications, I filed the appeal, with the kind help of a neighbor who happens to be an attorney, and duly received an acknowledgment. After several weeks I was invited to come in for an interview, where I was persuaded to withdraw the appeal in exchange for a nine-month further extension, during which time I could still pursue job opportunities and, if successful, apply for a renewed work permit.

Ironically, this book, warts and all, could be accepted (in lieu of a Swiss wife or relative) as the *Beziehung* or 'connection' to Switzerland which, along with sufficient funds, would permit me to retire here once I turn sixty, in January, 1998. Or, if I finally win a job that proves secure, I will eventually be granted a 'C' permit.

In the meantime, on Friday, 13th December, the local press reported a renewal of unemployment benefits of up to seven months beginning in January for anyone whose benefits had been *ausgesteuert*, exhausted, in 1996. I

---

exhibit: to display the wonders of embalming! 'Clarence's' fingernails were quite blue by then.

immediately made an appointment at the appropriate unemployment office to determine if I would qualify for such renewed benefits if I were to remain unemployed past the end of the year. If so, I would have automatically been granted a corresponding extension of my 'work' permit. The answer, however, was negative as my *Rahmenfrist*, or two-year time frame, had elapsed.

Despite reservations about the ethical aspects of the Swiss stock exchange's business practices, which are discussed in Chapter Four, I had applied for a position there on the suggestion of an acquaintance whom I chanced upon while hiking through the forest between Pfannenstiel and Meilen, but I was quickly refused employment. With the support of my colleague, I immediately appealed the decision, but was again denied consideration.

That left one application, with a foreign bank, still pending. The first signs looked promising: an interview with the two top officers went well, as did further conversations. I was encouraged – falsely, as it turned out – that my prospective superior, whose last name is Larue, laughed when I accidentally called him Mr. LaRouche; the Lyndon of that surname had been mentioned on CNN the previous evening. Even better, he did not seem at all perturbed when I mentioned that I had won an age discrimination case in the U.S. But then discussions were suspended just before Christmas – not, as I feared, because of my lack of specific experience in European markets, but because neither the Zürich office nor the foreign headquarters wanted to incur the salary expense.

In March, however, with the firm's expansion into stocks listed on the NASD, or National Association of Securities Dealers, in the U.S., discussions resumed, but then lapsed into oblivion again. I persisted, and in early May this benign neglect metamorphosed into an admission that no internal position would be forthcoming and a vague commitment (with even more nebulous results a month later) to recommend my candidacy to two client portfolio managers and one bank. By mid-June, no progress had been made or seemed likely. Larue seems to have had a Latin sense of time.

By April, fortunately, I had begun talks with two Swiss investors who are partners in several interlinked financial firms. One partner's entities distribute mutual funds both directly and through a Düsseldorf broker, and the other's underwrite new U.S. public issues for European investors and deal in foreign exchange. I was even taken to lunch – a rare sign of favor – at the *Wirtschaft Alter Tobelhof* at the edge of the forest above Stettbach. A perennial optimist, I was sanguine about the prospects, though aware of the irony that even then it might still be easier to secure employment here than in San Francisco.

I felt a few misgivings when I learned that many of the firms' clients were offshore corporations registered in Hong Kong or the Bahamas and controlled by Americans, and that most of the ten or so firms in which these partners are involved are also of the offshore variety. Moreover, I discovered, most of the five underwriting deals marketed to date have involved unregistered securities which cannot be legally owned by U.S. citizens or by foreigners domiciled in the U.S. Essentially, I suspected, by recommending such investment vehicles (whether or not in my role an analyst I considered them to be attractive situations) I would be helping my fellow countrymen avoid U.S. taxes. This I was initially reluctant to do, but when asked the firms' U.S. law firm blessed my assignment.

That legal opinion diminished my discomfort for having already corrected the abominable English of one such report as a 'test' of my writing skills. When I was asked to supply a disk of this edited report, I realized that the tieless senior partner intended to distribute it to clients and this impression was reinforced when he finally mentioned that he preferred to pay me by the piece rather than contractually commit himself to a standard salary and bonus arrangement. So, by way of compensating for my feeling of having been used, and in order to signal same, I sent him a bill for one and a half days' work at my most recent rate of salary, aware of the risk that discussions might be immediately terminated. Instead, I received a commitment to compensate me for such work and was immediately given a second assignment, which I performed within a forty-eight hour deadline.

Contract discussions then began. I was to receive a salary from the Swiss company and a commission 'off the books' (i.e. under the table) each time a deal was successfully completed. Such commissions, based not on any contractual obligation but rather on trust, would be paid by bearer check drawn upon an account owned by one of the offshore companies, and these amounts would not be included in the annual earnings statement supplied in duplicate to the tax authorities and to me. According to a prospective colleague, whose summer work outfit consists of a T-shirt and slacks, the combined firms' only female employee, a secretary, is also paid in this manner, and initially for his own benefit the Swiss company only recently established a pension plan, administered at a highly competitive price by the large German insurance company, Allianz.

I asked several trusted Swiss friends about the legality of such arrangements and all of them said, in effect, not to worry; in continental Europe, tax evasion is a gentleman's peccadillo, a *Cavaliers Delicto*. To her apparent credit, the German professor of law who lives in my apartment building advised me to be very careful about any such arrangement, but I cannot avoid the probably paranoid suspicion that no German would be entirely displeased to see an American expelled from Switzerland.

An American, of course, is obliged to report all earned income not only to the Swiss authorities but also to the U.S. Internal Revenue Service, and I am unwilling to evade either of these duties. Although my pointed questions may have conveyed this sentiment, discussions did continue, an offer was made and accepted, and I left for a vacation in the U.S. confidently expecting the promised contract to arrive in the mail. Instead, several weeks later, I received a letter advising me that it had been decided not to hire another analyst, but repeating the commitment to pay me for the work I had performed and asking for my exact address – which, complete to the inn's postal box number (previously unknown to me) had been derived from a computerized directory and appeared in the letter and on its envelope. I responded, but no payment was forthcoming.

Resolved to be paid for the four days' work I performed and to be reimbursed for related expenses, I turned the matter over to the attorney whom Credit Suisse had retained in 1989 to secure my initial work permit. He wrote the firm a letter threatening legal action if appropriate payment were not immediately forthcoming. No reply has been received, and the threat was a bluff: it is quite expensive to mount a lawsuit in Switzerland, and there is no contingency fee structure for lawyers. Nonetheless, I referred the matter to a second attorney, one unconnected with Credit Suisse and prominent in the small Swiss-Jewish community, and also to the Swiss employment office which may be interested in the demonstrated violation of the principle of *treu und glauben*, full faith and credit, which normally prevails.

No reply has been made by the employment office. The attorney, Sigi Feigel, whom I think of as 'Sig the Fig' or

'Siggy Figgy',[4] declined to intervene, and a third attorney advised me to forget the matter because my documentation was not letter-perfect. Moral: a foreigner cannot successfully sue a Swiss national in Switzerland.

Nonetheless, I persisted, and in mid-March I was finally paid an appropriate sum by the gentleman in question, a former partner of the Herr Kopp whose wife is mentioned later in this chapter. Surnamed Ernst, which means 'serious', 'earnest', he clearly had an earnest desire not to remunerate me.

Had I undertaken the position, it was my firm intention to report all income received to the tax authorities in both Switzerland and the U.S., a course of action which would doubtless have differentiated me, at least with regard to Switzerland, from at least two of the firm's employees, will keep me within the law, and will probably not endanger either of the partners.

In fairness, I should note that the first report's subject company, ComTelco, did look like an interesting, reasonably valued investment. Supported by such telephone hardware manufacturers as Alcatel, Ericsson, and Philips, the firm rationalizes centrex, billing and access arrangements for small to medium sized firms by providing appropriate software.

I should also acknowledge that the sample report I was shown, written by a California couple named Kohlhaas, concerned a registered company, SwissRay, which had engineered a reverse merger into a NASDAQ-listed shell; the company, which specializes in filmless digital x-rays, also has significant support from Philips and seemed attractive. Its headquarters, however, are in the same suite of offices as my prospective employer's companies, suggesting that he is a director of SwissRay who stood to

---

[4] *Feige* and *Feigling* also signify 'cowardly' and 'coward', respectively.

benefit from the financing he arranged in his investment banker's capacity.

However, when I happened to mention the name 'SwissRay' to my personal physician, who helps to direct an institute providing free x-rays to poor patients, he reacted quite negatively. It seems that, with the canton's approval, he and his colleagues inquired whether the company could provide a direct digital machine configured in a specific way, and was given positive assurances; but the desired machine turned out not to exist. 'It was a sham,' the internist told me in his excellent English. He advised caution. As though confirming his impressions, subsequent reports carried stronger disclaimers – e.g. 'This report contains statements believed to be correct but that cannot be guaranteed as to their accuracy...'[5]

Interestingly, the location of the office building housing these companies is known by the same name as the one Swiss investment company in the group. Possibly the building is at least partially owned by the very same entrepreneur who fills it with interrelated activities, or perhaps he simply named the company after an existing building. It would not be in good form to ask him which, if either, of these suppositions is accurate, or why his business stationery carries the letterhead of one of his firms but no address, telephone number, fax or telex.

After receiving the notification that, in effect, the oral contract would not be honored, I tried one last, desperate ploy to secure employment: I wrote to Dr. Dellsperger at Credit Suisse, once again describing my plight and suggesting that it would be good public relations for that institution to rehire me and thus avoid the expulsion from Switzerland of a Jewish American at a time when Swiss

---

[5]In March, 1998, I am reliably informed, SwissRay belatedly introduced a filmless digital model.

profiteering from the Holocaust was becoming increasingly controversial. I also reminded him (again) that the bank had rehired a fiftyish Japanese (I refrained from using the expression 'yellow Aryan') analyst named Kazuo Araki after he burned out at Nomura Securities. (Of course, Kazuo had a French-Swiss wife and a daughter, and had attained dual nationality.) This letter actually elicited a reply, but not a response to the religious issue: no positions were available, but the good doctor assured me that he sympathized with my situation and wished he could help.

At any rate, since none of my other soundings produced a job offer, I was forced to embrace the even more painful, if more honorable, alternative to joining this firm. Sans book or job, and lacking any specific destination, I had no choice but to bow to the authorities' edict and leave Switzerland, no doubt to make room for a Tamil, Turk, Yugoslav or African. This outcome, which took place within the 30th September deadline given me by the foreigners' police, may well be responsible for a certain amount of subconscious 'sour grapes' in this account.

I confess, also, that my own ingrained selectivity may have accounted, at least in part, for my wariness. The three positions that I've held with marked success – including my job at Credit Suisse – were all with mainstream companies which, in addition to their willingness to hire women in professional capacities, all shared certain elements, primarily an atmosphere that permitted easy bantering and exchanges of humor amid hard, productive work. Let me illustrate this with four negative examples.

In my prolonged transition from university teaching to investment analysis nearly thirty years ago, I once interviewed a textbook editor at Macmillan who was, shall we say, a flagrant flower. Unable to avoid noticing scores of highly attractive and desirable women in the department, I asked him how he was able to concentrate. His immediate boss, John Johnson, after hearing of this remark, dismissed me with a smile and a 'Well…'

In the early 1970s, I applied for an investment position with Unionmutual in Portland, Maine, and soon received from the personnel officer a form which asked me, among other things, to list my personal values. Helpful hints such as family, service to others and patriotism were given. My iconoclasm aroused by the conviction that no one so thoroughly conventional could possess the insight and independent thinking necessary to invest successfully, I put down materialism and personal development. Subsequently, the official wrote that he did not perceive a good fit between me and the company, but that he appreciated my having taken the time to fill out the form.

In the autumn of 1980 I applied for a position with Fidelity, only to be swamped by the number of applicants freshly graduated from Harvard Business School. Subsequently, a financial magazine published a photograph of a top portfolio manager – who, unlike several of his colleagues who had interviewed me, had vetoed my application without even meeting me – standing outside the firm's headquarters on Devonshire Street with a vagrant walking past. I whipped off a letter telling him that I was pleased at least to have had the opportunity of seeing what he looked like; but who, I asked, was the chap wearing the suit?

Or take my interview with a broker liaison department at Bear Stearns' New York headquarters in the mid-1980s. Bob Morey, the institutional salesman in San Francisco whose client I was at the time, arranged an interview with the head of this unit, which, like Bob, was at the time entirely Irish-American. This interviewer had on his desk, in the place where most professionals keep a photograph of their family, a snapshot of a chimpanzee wearing a pink bonnet. Naturally, I asked him if that was his wife; he was not amused and the interview ended soon thereafter.

At any rate, I am eager to resume a professional life, and I even bought a suit from Herr Hägi and another from London House in anticipation of returning to the world of remunerated work. The setting will be the U.S., whither I returned, bypassing Cincinnati in favor of taking an apartment in my beloved Nantucket[6] (where I had spent the summer in a fruitless search for a specific American destination-cum-employment) and applying without success for local jobs as well as for investment positions elsewhere. The friendliness of the natives and tourists here is a refreshing contrast to the forbidding aspects of Switzerland; at restaurants – many of which offer prime ribs of beef, justly praised by Thackeray – one can often and easily converse with neighboring diners, some of whom even initiate a discussion. The local television cable company also brings in four classical FM stations!

And there is easy banter and humor. One T-shirt I have seen commemorated the infamous limerick which begins, 'There once was a man from Nantucket'. Another, designed for a six-month-old infant, declares, over a picture of a bicycle, 'I'm here because my mommy missed her cycle.' A third, which I saw worn by a young woman, asks, 'Is that a banana in your pocket, or are you glad to see me?'

I am surprised by the large number of adults who shuttle between cheap furnished rooms in summer and more decent rooms in winter, and who, well into their thirties and forties, never acquire furniture, not even a bed, evidently preferring to spend their discretionary funds on drink.

---

[6]One advantage of resettling in Massachusetts was the availability of heath insurance, which the state legislature (unlike its counterpart in Ohio) had recently ordered to be offered to all comers, without a physical examination or exclusion of any pre-existing illnesses.

Some aspects of the local economy are reminiscent of the Swiss economy. The Steamship Authority, like the Swiss telephone company, is authoritarian and monopolistic and its services are high-priced compared to those offered by the ferries that ply Long Island Sound. The local hardware store flies in two small planeloads of clerks each morning from Cape Cod, such help being simply unavailable on the island. And large numbers of Jamaican 'guest workers' come here for eight months of the year to serve as maids, cooks, buspersons[7] and grocery checkout cashiers or baggers. A typical Jamaican with two such jobs earns (exclusive of tips) about sixteen thousand U.S. dollars each season, which translates into four hundred and eighty thousand Jamaican dollars, as opposed to twenty thousand only two decades ago, and so each spring they arrive en masse in chartered and commercial airplanes.

Nantucket society is straitified by address. The local gentry, if not the nobility, are in residence along Dukes Road. Starbuck Avenue houses descendants of old whaling families, while offshoots of the Mayflower crowd have migrated to Pilgrim Road. The selectmen are at home on Crooked Lane. Cattlemen ride herd on Mooers Street, while the dairymen fill their buckets on Milk Street. The corpulent squeeze by on Broad Street. The hermaphrodites are clustered (but not cloistered) in Middlesex Court. Young virgins dwell on Cherry Street or Vestal Street. Lower priced prostitutes, or *hetairas* as they were known in ancient Greece, congregate along Beaver Street, while their more expensive sisters live on Easy Street. Joy Street and Shady Lane are the loci of the drug trade. Chinese-Americans dwell on Chin's Way. The landscapers are to be found on Gardiner Street. The police lurk in Copper Lane, entrapping the denizens of Lily Street, while the

---

[7]But never as waitpersons.

counterfeiters congregate in New Dollar Lane. Lovers' Lane is frequented not by lovers but by drinkers, as it is the site of one of this small island's eight liquor stores. The infirm lie in Toombs Court, while those encumbered by heavy mortgage debt are concentrated along Long Pond Drive, whose road signs are occasionally repainted by one of their number to read Long Bond Drive. And you can guess the demographics of Coon Street.[8]

But let me return to my summary of the positives and negatives of that charming, alluring, elusive land that is Switzerland.

Swiss society works beautifully. The Swiss are trusting and are naturally inclined to trust you, and in many individual cases to be kind and considerate. They will remember your name and your preferences. Your innkeeper's wife, once she knows you, will not count the money you hand her as a deposit toward the bill if you simultaneously tell her how much it is. She will make a reservation on your word, or, at most, signature. A TV rental shop will deliver a set after you have looked the owner in the eyes and requested one. A pharmacy will give you prescription medicine on the strength of appropriate insurance identification and your word that the doctor will confirm the medication on the next business day. Bills follow weeks or – especially when sent by doctors – months after services have been rendered. Clerks disappear before you have paid for your purchase. The postal clerk runs your bills through the computer before you have demonstrated the means to pay them. There is little litigiousness. Streets and roads are kept in perfect repair. Trains and buses run on time, and their picture windows are invariably spotless, even in wet weather.

---

[8]Coon is of course, a Portuguese surname. Did you think I meant something else? Shame on you!

Although people are happy, thin and healthy, they still smoke far too much, thanks to American advertising about the macho Marlboro man and the like. (Marlboro sponsors an outdoor movie festival in Zürich and other major cities in the summer; when I first saw it advertised I thought it was the Vermont chamber music festival from Marlboro College.) Ten thousand Swiss die annually from diseases attributed to smoking tobacco, compared with four hundred from drug abuse and eleven hundred from alcoholism.

The three main cultures – German, French, and Italian – do not clash. No one (except American tourists) shouts or loses his temper. I have never witnessed a fight, nor do I care to. Although virtually every household has at least one military gun (with sealed bullets which may not be used) and while additional armor and ammunition are readily available even to foreigners, there is little crime; I can think of only three sensational murders during the seven and a half years that I have lived here. Children ride their bicycles to school unmolested and park them, often unlocked, with their helmets tied to the handlebars; thefts are extremely rare.

Despite the current hubbub over the Swiss government's and banks' role in profiting from the Holocaust, I have never personally sensed any overt religious prejudice here, especially from the German-Swiss. The only two apparently anti-Semitic remarks that I *have* heard came from Italians who nonetheless work for Jewish or highly integrated organizations. (Upon meeting me, the head of the Zürich office of the private bank for which I eventually worked did remark that I sounded very American; why didn't I go back to New York and seek a job there?) Despite my Aryan appearance – with blue eyes and blond hair, I have twice been mistaken for Boris Becker, who is half my age and plays far better tennis – my own

Jewish background (briefly eclipsed when I experimented with the Anglican faith in the late 1960s; not unlike at least one Anglican archbishop, I kept stumbling over the Nicene creed) is inferred from my surname by many educated Swiss, who sometimes allude to their awareness of it, but this has been much less of an issue than in Boston or San Francisco, parochial places where one needs two Harvard or Stanford degrees, and where it helps enormously to be named Adams, Cabot, Holbrook or Jones.(In the latter city, a salesman once criticized my alleged New York accent as unfit for the local investment community, and that Midwood character to whom I referred previously – himself a transplanted Bostonian – once advised me that the best career opportunities for someone of my background were to be found in New York. I lived there for sixteen years and loved it at the time, but have now become accustomed to more civilized cities.) At any rate, most institutions that I have encountered in Zürich do employ Jews in professional capacities.

Thus I do not attribute the possibility of being forced to leave Switzerland to anti-Jewish sentiment, and I resist the occasional temptation to think of myself, like a character in Herman Wouk's *The Winds of War*, as just another Jew on the verge of being expelled from continental Europe. (In any case, although my status as a resident may soon end, I plan to return as a tourist, and to leave my skiing equipment in Klosters and Zermatt. They can kick me out of Switzerland, but they can't purge Switzerland from my soul.)

On the other hand, in a country in which the head of a large bank (Union Bank of Switzerland) bragged to *The New Yorker's* Jane Mayer that with one possible exception there were no Jews in the top managements of the three largest banks, it would not be prudent or useful to mention the fact that three of my ancestors were *prominenti*. My great uncle, Bernard Revel, founded Yeshiva University in New York and, many years later, his likeness was depicted on a U.S. commemorative postage stamp. My uncle, Nelson Glueck, a well-known Biblical scholar, archaeologist, author, seminary president and cleric, discovered King Solomon's copper mines by literally translating the Hebrew Bible's account of their location; and, in January, 1961, he gave the benediction at John Fitzgerald Kennedy's presidential inauguration. My cousin, Carl Rubin (no relation to Jerry), was a federal district judge in Kentucky until his recent death.

Nor would it be relevant to confide to a Swiss friend that four of my maternal grandfather's siblings probably perished at Auschwitz; poor shtetl Jews all, they are not remotely likely to have held among them even one Swiss bank account.

On a less personal note, I doubt that the Swiss will approve their federal leadership's proposal to monetize forty tons of gold reserves for the benefit of human rights causes. So far, the controversy about this proposal is quiet, notwithstanding reports of politicians and even individual Swiss Jews receiving threatening letters often signed by their senders. The vast majority of the Swiss appear indifferent to the issue, apolitical, secular. About the only visible reactions are the awakenings of dormant anti-Semitism implied in such televised comments as 'Why should we repay the Jews? They already have too much money,' or 'President Clinton's Middle Eastern policy is not evenhanded: he attacks Iraq but implicitly condones Israel's possession of nuclear weapons.' Old, exploded stereotypes die hard.

I have seen graffiti proclaiming 'Nazis, raus' – from what provocation, I have no idea – but never 'Juden raus.' The last known cell of Nazi sympathizers was dissolved in Davos six decades ago. No synagogues have been attacked in Switzerland, despite the nervousness of congregants who generally monitor a closed-circuit television screen during religious services. The commercial instinct reigns supreme; no shop owner, at least in my experience, ever refuses to do business with even the most obvious Lubavitch or Chasidic varieties of orthodox Jews.

According to Robert Lesser, a retired Swiss journalist who converted from Judaism to Methodism half a century ago and who once worked for Credit Suisse, the Swiss may not welcome Jews with open arms (as they do, for example, Kurt Waldheim, whom I have seen at the Tonhalle) or even like them very much, and they may have closed their borders to Jewish immigrants during the Nazi era, but no Jewish citizen of Switzerland was ever deported 'to the east' or anywhere else, for that matter.

Yet, although they may not share the racist fantasies still proclaimed by neo-Nazis in as nearby a city as Munich, the Swiss are not totally uninfected by the old Nazi racial stereotypes, as my former Credit Suisse supervisor, Bruno Guldener, once acknowledged. Harvard Professor Daniel Jonah Goldhagen, in his acclaimed book *Hitler's Willing Executioners*, characterizes the prevailing Nazi German view of Jews as parasitic work shirkers who live off others' labor and who, like Shylock,[9] lend money at usurious rates; as

---

[9] Shylock's character, of course, was influenced by the prevalence of the very stereotypes that he has come to exemplify. 'I am', he declares, 'a Jew. Hath not a Jew eyes? hath not a Jew hands, organs, dimensions, senses, affections, passions? fed with the same food, hurt with the same weapons, subject to the same diseases, healed by the same means, warmed and cooled by the same winter and summer, as a Christian is? If you prick us, do we not bleed? if you tickle us, do we not laugh? if you poison us, do we not die? and if you wrong us, shall we not revenge? if we are like you in the rest, we will resemble you in that. If a Jew wrong a Christian, what is his humility? Revenge. If a Christian wrong a Jew, what should his sufferance be by Christian example? Why, revenge. The villainy you teach me I will execute, and it shall go hard but I will better

hypermaterialistic, dishonest, and thievish amassers of wealth stolen from the *Volk* (Michael Milken is thought by many Swiss to exemplify this last 'racial' characteristic); and as scheming evildoers who stir up trouble and internecine strife within otherwise harmonious communities. Thus a foreign Jew who becomes unemployed and claims his social welfare benefits can be judged more harshly than his Christian counterpart in the same predicament. I am reminded of Massachusetts voters' sudden turning against black Senator Ed Brooke after he allegedly committed the heinous sin of understating his financial position during an acrimonious divorce proceeding.

Against these perceptions, it is worth noting that President Clinton chose to name a Jewish woman, Madeleine Kunin, as ambassador to Switzerland, and that the Swiss federation's ruling council includes another Jewish woman, Ruth Dreifuss, who was born in Endingen, one of three contiguous towns near Aarau where not too many generations ago Jews were forced to live, and where their choices of occupation were largely limited to trading cattle and farming. Mrs. Dreifuss replaced a controversial Christian woman who shocked the political elders by going bra-less and wearing dungarees.

(Another prominent female politician here, Elizabeth Kopp, was forced out of office after being accused – and tried, with the result an acquittal – of breaching government secrets by warning her businessman husband to avoid dealing with a controversial figure. A woman entering Swiss politics has about as much chance as Ed Brooke had.)

Even those Swiss who harbor no overt racial or religious prejudices remain, by and large, *ein verschlossenes Volk*, a

the instruction. William Shakespeare, *The Merchant of Venice*, Act III, Scene I.

closed society. Perhaps in part because of this, all too often the resident foreigner cannot help feeling that the German-Swiss – especially the Zürichoise – lean and athletic though they be, are two-dimensional caricatures of human beings, highly venal and mercenary, lacking souls. Italians and even some Germans can offer a welcome contrast.

In eight years of living here, I have met only one truly desirable woman, Rebekka, a beautiful, full-bodied assistant at the private bank where I formerly worked. Rebekka is fully human, with the loveliest face in Switzerland, derived from her Italian-Swiss mother; unfailingly friendly; trilingual; an exquisite singer and pianist who studied piano under Bruno Leonardo Gelber and attends (but does not give) concerts and recitals; happily wedded to the only boyfriend she has ever known, also Italian-Swiss, whom she met when she was fifteen and married at thirty – fortunately, not too late to give birth to a little Rebekka.

As you can gather, on a scale of one to ten my chances of winning Rebekka were less than zero. I must confess, probably not to your surprise by now, that I have never been intimate with a Swiss woman. (Yes, I am thoroughly heterosexual.) Except for Rebekka, they all fail the following screen: Does she refrain from smoking? Wear pastels instead of black? Shave her legs and under her arms? Read, attend classical concerts, play an instrument, sing seriously, or show other signs of education and culture? Is she interested in loving me for me alone, as the song in *Annie* goes, or does she infer from my clothes or car that I am wealthy enough to support her in the style to which she wishes to become accustomed? Is she *too* available? I suspect, à la Groucho Marx, that any woman who is prepared to jump into bed with me on brief acquaintance is not very discriminating.

I did try once. I dated an attractive woman named Susie who owns a small house in Zollikon, which borders

Zürich. Susie wears black cashmere sweaters with black wool skirts, along with a Rolex. Her boss, she told me, brought written permission from his wife for her to sleep with him; unlike his previous secretaries, she claims, she refused, but she accepts a daily good morning kiss, money toward the purchase of a new car and 'invitations' to play tennis with him most sunny afternoons. She once sent me a postcard from Bahrain, where she had been invited to join a trio of male Swiss businessmen in order, she says, to make a fourth at bridge which, as well as tennis, she teaches. She has never been married. I danced with her once, and noticed the absence of deodorant. My freshly dry-cleaned suit absorbed a stench that required hours of hanging outside on the terrace to clear.

Even if you are far less fastidious than I am, some cultural differences will certainly appall you. When you go to a swimming area you will see topless women, some wearing thongs, some not even that much. Ah, you think, how nice! (*Ne 'tush' pas!*) Then the object of your admiration raises her arm. Ugh! Shaving of body hair is not universal here. And there are lots of *Hängetitten*, as aerobic exercises are virtually unknown. Jane Fonda, the Swiss need your videocassettes! In the course of a summer, with women changing into and out of bathing suits all around me without benefit of a towel, I see perhaps three truly beautiful female bodies, perhaps one face hinting at a compassionate soul within.

In such circumstances, as at office parties, you are likely to feel like an observer, a tourist, rather than a participant. Occasionally, you will see someone whom you know, perhaps a neighbor and his topless wife. The first time this happens, you will have to summon all your savoir-faire not to blush or be nervous and to look the woman in the eyes, not the nipples – unless, of course, you come from

California or Florida, or perhaps Vermont or Martha's Vineyard.[10]

Manners are not important to the Swiss. Motorists will seldom stop for you at crosswalks, which indeed in Zürich are being eliminated for precisely that reason. As I have already noted, colleagues will almost never introduce you to their families if you happen to encounter them. People seem to time their coughs and sneezes to occur just as you come within range, and they rarely cover their noses and mouths effectively, if at all. Pedestrians as well as drivers will maneuver to get in front of you so that they can then slow down and block you. People often stop at the top of a flight of stairs or, especially, an escalator and obstruct the egress.

In general, you will often be made to feel that you do not exist or are invisible, like a little boy standing at the edge of a school yard watching the trams back up and turn around at the end of the line while a few yards away his classmates play a boisterous game of 'baseball' with a tennis ball, oblivious to his feelings of rejection upon not being chosen for either team. If only he had been the one child who remembered to bring a ball to school that day! He would keep it in his pocket until the end of the recess and then take it out and bounce it ostentatiously to show the others that it is he who rejects them. But in Switzerland it is never your ball or your field. As Paul Erdman notes in his book *The Swiss Account*, it is impossible to get close to the Swiss – especially when they deliberately speak their local dialect rapidly so that you cannot understand what they are saying. Only those with a well-deserved inferiority complex

---

[10]The Swiss are not inhibited or shocked when it comes to obscene language broadcast on radio or television. Swiss disc jockeys, restaurants, and ski areas regularly play Gompie's unexpurgated version of the English rock group Smokie's song, *Living Next Door to Alice*, which features the refrain, 'Who the fuck is Alice?'

would choose to be so peculiar in their language and customs.

The ugliest and most arrogant Swiss live in Zürich. Plastic surgery to correct hook noses is practically unknown, and there are lots of highly unattractive noses. The most mercenary Swiss also live in Zürich. The odds are quite high that any conversation you overhear while walking along the *trottoir* or sidewalk will be about money, with lots of numbers mentioned frequently. On trains, you will hear a lot of talk about train schedules. *Dusig*, by the way, is Swiss German for *tausend*, 'thousand'; *zah* for *zehn* or 'ten.' And *adee* means adieu.

Appendix
EEOC Documentation of Civil Rights Violation

Determination

Under the authority vested in me by the Commission, I issue the following determination as to the merits of the subject charge filed under The Age Discrimination in Employment Act of 1967, as amended (ADEA).

All requirements for coverage have been met. Charging Party alleged that Respondent discriminated against him and engaged in an unlawful employment practice in violation of the ADEA, by maintaining a policy of not considering candidates over the age of 33, and by failing to consider his application because of his age (57).

The evidence shows that Charging Party is a 58-year old American male who at age 57 applied for a position as a… with… Charging Party applied for employment in or around April of 1995, by submitting his unsolicited résumé to Respondent's Swiss office. He was subsequently informed, by letter dated May 4, 1995, that Respondent does not consider applicants who are over the age of 33. When he appealed this decision, Respondent confirmed its policy in a second letter dated May 15, 1995, and denied him an interview.

The evidence confirms that Respondent denied Charging Party an interview based on its policy, because he was over the age of 33. Respondent explained in the first letter that according to the firm's experience, older applicants encounter difficulties adapting to its environment and working with a considerably younger team. Respondent also stated that career opportunities for such candidates were limited.

The record shows that none of Respondent's hires in 1995 was over age 33.

The record clearly shows that Respondent maintained a policy of not hiring anyone over age 33, that Respondent made no exception to this policy, and that the policy adversely affected the Charging Party in his consideration for employment. Based on this analysis, I have determined that there is reasonable cause to believe that the Respondent violated the ADEA.

The ADEA requires that, if the Commission determines that there is reason to believe that a violation has occurred, it shall endeavor to eliminate the alleged unlawful employment practice by informal methods of conference, conciliation, and persuasion. Having determined that there is reason to believe that a violation has occurred, the Commission now invites the Respondent to join with it in a collective effort toward a just resolution of this matter. A representative of this office will be in contact with the Respondent in the near future to begin the conciliation process with respect to the ADEA violation.

Disclosure of information obtained by the Commission during the conciliation process will be made in accordance with the statute and Section 1601.26 of the Commission's Procedural Regulations. If the Respondent declines to enter into settlement discussions, or when, for any other reason, the Commission's representative is unable to secure a settlement acceptable to the office Director, I will so inform the Respondent in writing of the court enforcement alternative of the Commission.

On behalf of the Commission,

December 5, 1996   (signed)
                          District Director

Enclosure (1):
Information Sheet on Filing
Suit in Federal Court

0-595-24171-9

Lightning Source UK Ltd.
Milton Keynes UK
02 March 2010

150832UK00001B/46/A